HOW TO LIVE WITH A
UNICORN

The Fantastic Guide to
Keeping Mythical Pets

JANE MOSELEY

Ivy Press

First published in the UK in 2007 by

Ivy Press
The Old Candlemakers
West Street, Lewes
East Sussex, BN7 2NZ, UK
www.ivy-group.co.uk

British Library Cataloguing-in-Publication Data
A catalogue record for this book is available from the British Library

ISBN 10: 1-905695-34-9
ISBN 13: 978-1-905695-34-8

Ivy Press
This book was conceived,
designed, and produced by
iBall, an imprint of Ivy Press

CREATIVE DIRECTOR Peter Bridgewater
PUBLISHER Jason Hook
EDITORIAL DIRECTOR Caroline Earle
SENIOR PROJECT EDITOR Dominique Page
ART DIRECTOR Sarah Howerd
DESIGNER James Lawrence
ILLUSTRATOR Tonwen Jones
CONCEPT DESIGN Tonwen Jones

Printed and bound in China

Acknowledgments
*Huge thanks to smaller, but equally fabulous, monsters who inspired
the author: (in order of size) Harry, Ted, Twiggy, Cino, and Ginger.*

CONTENTS

INTRODUCTION

It's raining cats and dogs in the world of pet-keeping, but you don't see many minotaurs or gorgons falling from the sky. Think of this book as a guide to taking your first step along the challenging, but exciting, path to owning a fantastic pet. You will end up with a companion that not even your most aspirational neighbors could dream of, let alone house. Step outside and see how many basilisks perched on white picket fences, or sirens peering over them, you can see in your area. You won't just be keeping up with the Joneses—you will be snapping at their heels or biting big chunks out of their petfolios.

Here you will find a careful selection of fabulous pets, including two-legged, four-legged, one-, three-, and nine-headed, hairy, scaly, furry, feathered, leonine, bovine, hybrid, and part-human. This book highlights key facts regarding the origin, character, and appearance of all the pets in the lineup, telling you what you need to know in order to provide the right creature comforts, correct diet, and appropriate veterinary care. It also outlines just how much fun you can have together.

Think carefully before making your final choice. Sadly, rescue shelters are full of pets whose owners have regretted decisions made in haste. Consider with care your environment—its location, dimensions, and facilities. Urban apartment-owners and elephant-carrying birds, for example, will find arrangements particularly challenging. Likewise, try squeezing an adult dragon into a motorhome and things could get dangerously overcrowded and overheated. Examine your budget. Can you afford to keep a satyr in wine or a bunyip in fresh claws? Think closely about your social life, too. Can you risk losing what friends you have by asking a basilisk to share your life? Investigate your motives. Do you hanker after a yeti just so you can say you have seen one? Do you fancy a harpy only

because you could do with a few free meals? And don't go on looks alone. A unicorn is beautiful but very demanding, and you can't buy virgins at the drop of a hat nowadays. Think about your personality, which pet might suit your character most, and examine your motives for choosing a particular pet. For instance, do you have the patience for a sphinx with its endless riddles? Crossword puzzles would be much less taxing. Those with bipolar tendencies will find a minotaur pulls them in too many directions. Schizophrenics will discover that a leucrotta won't help solve their dilemma. Aquaphobics will learn that a mermaid won't get them off the couch. Intellectuals looking for mental stimulation will soon tire of an ogre.

Once you have pinpointed your perfect pet, invest time in locating a reputable breeder. Don't take the easy route of placing a loosely worded advertisement in the local newspaper. "Man with fertile imagination seeks fairy," "Undomesticated male seeks selkie wife," or "Lovelorn lady with appetite for revenge needs lamia" will attract frauds and fly-by-nights. You may not end up with the real thing and there is

nothing more disappointing than a pegasus that cannot fly or more dangerous than a cerberus with no pedigree. Head to the library, municipal or virtual, and research authentic sources.

Finding the right supplier should not be left to chance—it is too hit and myth; ask for the supplier's history and credentials, for photographs or detailed descriptions, and for references from fellow contented owners. If a breeder promises several for a phoenix, he or she is not for real.

Now that you have all the preliminary information at your (very well-protected) fingertips, prepare to find out more about your potential pet.

It's gloves-off stuff …

FOUR-LEGGED PETS

All four feet of these quadrupeds are present, but not always grounded. The unicorn is out of this world, as are the hippogriff and pegasus. The cerberus is very down to earth, while the leucrotta has two feet firmly in two camps.

How to live with a ...

UNICORN

*Y*ou like rarity and you will put up with a lot to attain it. As soon as someone else has that elusive pink pearl or that ocean-going yacht, your own loses all luster. You don't just want special, you want unique, even unattainable. If this is you, then you should consider a unicorn. Ethereal, yet wild, beautiful, yet fierce, it has special requirements but is nothing if not exclusive. Its startling appearance will make your neighbors gasp, and its challenging character, once tamed, will deliver a real sense of achievement.

• Unicorn
(Unicornis Virginibus)

Appearance
Exquisite. The pure-white body of the most refined thoroughbred horse with a mane, hooves, and twisted horn of the purest, gleaming silver. Unlike a horse, it has a leonine tassel of a tail, and cloven goatlike hooves. The unicorn is tougher than it looks, but its looks are very delicate indeed.

Character
Despite its extraordinarily refined looks, the unicorn has a naturally fierce and implacable temperament and, if you are unlucky enough to annoy it, it can inflict serious damage with teeth, hooves, and horn. Don't even think about riding it! It was first documented in medieval bestiaries and allegedly originated in India. Over the centuries it

became a byword for purity: impure things offend and make it cross (hence the need for virgins, see below). Early manuals attribute a strong musical sense to the unicorn, although sources are divided as to whether it sings or prefers to listen. A musical soiree or two will reveal the truth.

What you need

• **Plenty of virgins.** Unicorns can be fed, groomed, and handled only by a young and beautiful virgin. Modern mores and morals sadly mean that even if you recruit one, there is no guarantee that he or she will keep the status in the long term. If you are not yourself a lovely virgin, be prepared to interview frequently and maintain a constant backup.

• **A substantial piece of private woodland.** Unicorns exercise at night and, in addition to a good diet, require moonlight to keep their coats in top gleam.

• **A highly developed aesthetic sense.** Unicorns are a challenge to maintain, so there's really no point in having one unless you have a wide repertoire of troubadour's ballads up your romantic, trailing sleeve to go with it.

Interviews
You'll need a constant supply of virgins. Male owners might enjoy the question-and-answer process, after overcoming the initial embarrassment.

" *The ideal companion for the seasoned poseur.* "

Feeding habits

These are fairly straightforward. The unicorn grazes at night, in moonlit glades. Regular, well-tended grass will meet its basic energy needs, and moonlight will keep its coat in top condition. Unicorns are very sensitive and easily put off their food, so you must ensure that its grazing ground is well secured and as remote as possible from any possible intruders. Poaching is, sadly, a risk, as the horn and blood of unicorns repel poison and are therefore somewhat desirable, but, on the plus side, this special gift means that any impurities the unicorn might ingest while grazing are prevented from infecting its system.

Veterinary care

Despite their delicate appearance, unicorns are actually famously strong, and it would take a great deal to inflict serious harm upon them. Should your unicorn manage to contract anything serious, a virgin veterinarian will be required to tend to it; no horny-handed practitioners will be able to handle it. Silver polish and oil are needed to maintain the lovely luster of the unicorn's horn and hooves.

Companion pets

Few other pets will make suitable friends for the unicorn, which is by nature somewhat remote and self-contained. However, if your dedicated woodland includes a deep pool, you might consider a mermaid. It is possible that these two equally exquisite creatures might make music together, and they will certainly make an aesthetically appealing couple. That other music-lover, the shapeshifting selkie, could strike the right note under a virgin moon. Don't consider a centaur: it will prove too robust a companion for the refined unicorn.

Fun things to do with your unicorn

- *Housework—perhaps not our favorite activity, but the horn magically cleans everything it touches.*

- *Pose—this ultimate eye-catcher will trigger lots of "oohing" and "aahing" whenever you take a twilight walk together.* Dungeons and Dragons *enthusiasts may want to dress up to achieve the full romantic effect.*

- *Distinguish base from precious metals—your pet can tell lead from gold. Practice a little, then rent your pet's time out to jewelers, miners, and other interested parties.*

Owner's qualification: postgrad in history and fashion.

Game on
If role play is your thing, then this pet will let your imagination run wild. Fantasy, fable, and folklore rolled into one. You win hands down.

How to live with a ...

HIPPOGRIFF

*I*f you are the sort of person who likes to have the best of both worlds, the hippogriff could have been tailor-made for you. It is the product of an unlikely union between a male griffin and a filly, so if split-split personalities intrigue you, read on. With grandparents on its father's side a mix of eagle and lion, the hippogriff provides an interesting exercise in pet genealogy, a great conversation piece, and some unusual family photographs.

Character

The hippogriff could be forgiven for being at worst schizophrenic, at best a little mixed up, given its background. Although it has a foot in each camp, at least two of them are firmly on the ground. It has the might, and no doubt the *coeur de lion*, of its father, the griffin, but not the same unbridled meanness. The magnificently powerful hippogriff can be tamed, saddled up, and enjoyed as the most environmentally-friendly form of air transport you could wish for. It makes a trusty steed and pet, and you will feel just like a knight in a Charlemagne legend aboard your fabulous aerial mount.

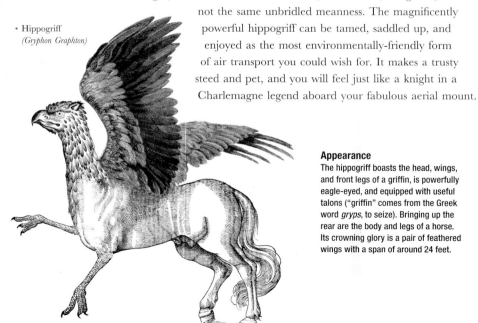

• Hippogriff
(Gryphon Graphton)

Appearance

The hippogriff boasts the head, wings, and front legs of a griffin, is powerfully eagle-eyed, and equipped with useful talons ("griffin" comes from the Greek word *gryps*, to seize). Bringing up the rear are the body and legs of a horse. Its crowning glory is a pair of feathered wings with a span of around 24 feet.

What you need

• **Large, custom-built accommodation.** Your architect will need to incorporate stable, nest, and aviary into a harmonious design.

• **Proximity to a mountain range.** The hippogriff learned to fly in the Riphaean Mountains in the frozen north of Europe and needs to return to keep its license up. Let it spread its wings.

• **A strong constitution.** You will be breaking the sound barrier at high altitude, and there's no hostess service or bathroom.

• **No favoritism.** You must love all aspects of your pet equally, and be a lion admirer, horse aficionado, and bird-fancier.

High flyer
For some, this pet equals the impossible. Even if pigs can't fly, the hippogriff can. Provide all it needs to take to the skies.

❝ A personal pet and eco-jet. ❞

Feeding habits

The term "herbinsectcarnivore" would best describe the hippogriff's tastes, but in the absence of such a word, omnivore will do. Bear in mind that its brain thinks like an eagle, but its stomach could eat like a horse. The ideal menu for the hippogriff would involve an hors d'oeuvre of plants, followed by a smorgasbord of rats and other small rodents, with a side dish of insects. Famous hippogriffs are said to enjoy a luxury diet of dead ferrets. The important thing is for it to take on board enough fuel for in-flight, take-off, and landing activities.

Veterinary care

You will need to find an interdisciplinary, multitasking veterinarian to attend to your hippogriff, one who specializes in avian, feline, and equine care. He or she will need to see your pet as a whole, appreciate the pecking order of its various physical demands, and be persuaded not to give it the bum's rush. Complementary, holistic medicines tend to work best, given its contradictory requirements. Your hippogriff will probably give your veterinarian a firm leg up if any treatments involve unrealistic flights of fancy.

Fun things to do with your hippogriff

- *Park it in a large, customized loose-box at a huge rock concert or Super Bowl event—make a swift airborne exit and watch the gridlock from above with a smug grin.*

- *Take it to a safari park and enjoy watching the lions' faces—their thunder well and truly taken as it flies overhead.*

- *Join a falconry club—any complaints about the unorthodox nature of your charge will be silenced when they see the size of the prey it can retrieve.*

Adult wingspan: approx. 23'.

Trophy pet
The hippogriff is a real winner—a post-ancient, open-to-the-elements private jet. Your life will well and truly take off when you land one.

Companion pets

It should come as no surprise to learn that the hippogriff's best friend and distant cousin is pegasus, the winged horse. They took advanced flying lessons together and like to compete in formation-flying displays at air shows. They make an impressive sight as they soar overhead. The hippogriff is much more adept at grasping the many trophies they win, but pegasus is able to complete a far more graceful victory trot. They take the give-and-take relationship to new heights, and correspond regularly, by airmail, of course.

How to live with a …

PEGASUS

*I*f you feel inclined toward a divine equine, then consider the mighty pegasus. It is a horse, for all intents and purposes, but no ordinary sort or breed. Winged and wise, it can trace its family tree way back to Ancient Greece, when the first wild pegasus, sired by Poseidon in his role as horse-god, leapt out of the recently removed head of the unfortunate snake-haired gorgon, Medusa. With a pedigree like that, pegasus isn't going to go home with just anyone.

• Pegasus
(Equus Equinus Divinus)

Appearance
Beauty is not simply in the eye of the beholder in this case. A magnificent white stallion of incredible beauty, pegasus sports a huge pair of powerful, sometimes golden, wings, a long, flowing tail, and crescent-moon-shaped hooves. Impressively large, but equally elegant, it is graceful on terra firma and when airborne. This is definitely no flight of fancy.

Character

Courageous, devoted, strong, and gentle, pegasus is a legend of a pet. The ancient pegasus had strong associations with the city of Corinth in Ancient Greece. Its ancestors took their riders on airborne—sometimes monster-slaying—adventures, but you can request much more peaceful journeys, even day trips, enjoying 360-degree views and no check-in lines. Pegasus is a superior pet both in visual appeal and character; it is pure, noble, loyal, and wise. However, if you have ideas above your station, you could be dropped by your pet unceremoniously —the Corinthian victor, Bellerophon, was unseated by pegasus on a high-flying attempt to reach the gods on Mount Olympus. You have been warned.

A heavenly pet for the high flyer.

What you need

• **A golden bridle.** Bellerophon needed one to tame his pegasus when he wanted to take it on its first airborne mission, and so will you. Take his lead. Approach your pet gently, cast the golden harness around its neck, and—voilà—one tamed horse. Climb aboard: the sky's the limit.

• **A strong moral code.** Pegasus likes to accomplish missions, turning evil into good wherever it can. You have to do the right thing; you can't just go along for the ride.

• **A talent for languages.** To communicate with your intelligent pet and become an impressive horse whisperer, you will need to find time to attend evening classes in its own mother tongue, Ancient Greek.

Feeding habits

Pegasus is a normal herbivorous, grazing horse, but is sometimes forced to eat on the hoof on in-flight journeys. After energetic pursuits, it likes to drink deliciously cool, refreshing water, but you won't be required to take it on board or even supply the source—it simply stamps at the ground when thirsty and where its hoof hits rock, a freshwater spring appears. The fountain of Hippocrene on Mount Helicon, sacred to the Muses, was the first to be created in this fashion by one of its ancestors, so named after the Greek *hippos* for horse and *krene* for fountain.

Veterinary care

Once tamed, most veterinarians will be honored to treat pegasus if it is feeling unwell. It requires regular baths (try milk and honey) and gentle brushing to retain its purity of color, and the golden-winged variety will need a weekly polish, too. You will also need to find yourself an expert farrier to look after its unique hooves. When elderly, you will be relieved to discover, Pegasus can enter the stable of the gods upon Olympus and spend a simply divine retirement there.

Recommended products: fulfilled cow organic milk and contented bee honey.

First-class travel
Your pet assures designer departures and arrivals for all its privileged private passengers. Your social life will take off.

Companion pets

Pegasus will enjoy spending time with the unicorn, deep in intellectual discussion about purity and goodness, and exchanging tips on how to stay whiter than white in an increasingly murky world. The hippogriff is its companion of choice for more physical pursuits and flying practice. Pegasus should be kept well away from the fire-breathing chimera—their ancestors were locked in battle during antiquity and the chimera came off distinctly worse.

Fun things to do with your pegasus

- *Enter the local dressage contest—you will clear every fence with as much ease as you lose jealous friends in the neighborhood.*

- *Take up poetry—due to its link with the Muses, it is said to inspire those who ride it to indulge in verse. Listen to your Muse, and learn to express your views, in charming, rhyming twos. Trust me, it could be a lot worse ...*

- *Next time you go to a chic party—make a dramatic entrance on horseback. When things get dull or out of hand, make a hasty airborne exit. Pegasus excels at vertical take-off and landing techniques and is perfect for the runway-free runaway.*

How to live with a ...

LEUCROTTA

*D*on't worry if you're finding it hard to picture your ideal pet—you should, perhaps, consider the leucrotta (also known as the leucocruta). Nature appears to have been up to some serious mischief when designing this particular creature, mixing stag, lion, and badger together on just four legs, then throwing in some extra features and serious body odor issues for good measure. Either that, or survival of the fittest took an unusual turn. You couldn't make it up.

Appearance
The size of a wild ass, the leucrotta sports the powerful haunches of a stag, the muscular torso and tail of a lion, the head of a badger, and four cloven hooves. Its mouth is slit as far back as its ears (all the better to eat you with) and, strangely, it lacks eyelids ...

Character
Pliny the Elder, the author and philosopher, way back in 77 CE, was among the first to bring our attention to this unusual pet. The leucrotta is no slouch. It may look like it was designed by a committee, but it must have been the one from Olympia. It is up there on the podium when medals for fastest land animals are handed out, but its temper is quick off the mark, too. Naturally fierce, it will need strict training. Make sure you show it who's boss or you will have a monster on your hands. And it can mimic the human voice, so always have the last word.

The ideal pet for those suffering from an identity crisis.

• Leucrotta
(Beastus Horribilis)

What you need

• **Mirror-lined accommodation for your pet.** Its back is so rigid that it has to turn around to see behind it. It might not like what it sees, but then who does? You could always try painting a trompe l'oeil featuring a unicorn.

• **A large scrubbing brush on a chainsaw.** The leucrotta has a large ridge of bone in both jaws of its gaping mouth instead of standard teeth. It can get up to its ears in plaque.

• **A supply of comforting eye masks.** Nature forgot to add the eyelids, so you will need to improvise. Help your pet get a bit more shut-eye overnight, thereby improving its temper and behavior. You should sleep better at night, too.

DIY dentals
Necessity is the mother of invention, in this case, the customized leucrotta toothbrush. Forget flossing or use a thin lasso.

Feeding habits

The leucrotta's diet is naturally mixed and can be somewhat demanding. The needs of the carnivorous hunter are easier to swallow when they are tempered by those of a rodent-eating badger at the front and the herbivorous stag at the back. Your pet will be able to procure its own entrée of voles, small mice, and ground squirrels, and can finish off with a refreshing pick 'n' mix, all-you-can-eat salad of leaves, fruit, and grasses, but it will need help to satisfy its leonine demands on the main-dish front, unless you live in a safari park populated by a plentiful supply of buffalo, zebra, and wildebeest.

Veterinary care

The leucrotta will be too demanding for your average veterinarian, so you will need to track down a willing specialist, one who enjoys working in the combined disciplines of small and large animals plus big game. Reassure your veterinarian that you have dental care covered and make sure that he or she attends on one of the days when the lion section is distracted by the digestion of a large animal. Extra precautions include both eye mask and large metal muzzle. If tempers flare, try a general anaesthetic (for your pet, not the vet).

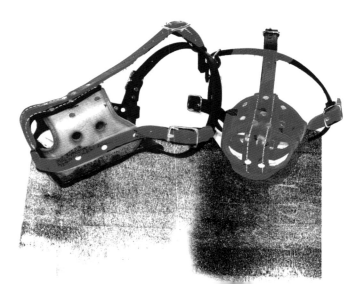

Buckle up
You may find a muzzle useful for visits by the local veterinarian or your consultant psychiatrist. You decide who gets to wear it.

Keep a lid on it
Don't let your pet badger you for too many buffalo. It can avail itself of small mammals and mixed greens with ease.

Recommended diet: strict vegetarian/ big game.

Companion pets

You would think that being part badger, stag, and lion would help your leucrotta make friends easily, at least with some of its parts. Sadly, for it, at least, its dental arrangements and mix 'n' match dress sense put many creatures off. It just isn't cool to be seen with, and you may be its only friend. You could try asking its parents, the crocottas, around for dinner, but they specialize in digging up the buried dead, so be prepared.

Fun things to do with your leucrotta

- *Take up a part-time job as a ventriloquist—the leucrotta's skill at mimicry is worth mentioning, whereas its capacity for sparkling dialog is nothing to speak of.*

- *Make an impact in a crowd—the quite intolerable body odor of the leucrotta will clear the way in any crowded place.*

- *Sponsor a local five-legged race for charity and enter your pet—it will win hands down, and who is going to challenge it for having only four legs?*

How to live with a …

CERBERUS

$\mathscr{Y}$ou don't favor lapdogs, and you've never gone in for bows, spaniel eyes, or a long, silky coat. The sort of canine that takes your fancy has been bred over generations as a lean, mean, killing machine. The dogs you've owned have boasted names to match: Fang, perhaps, or Terminator. Cerberus is your kind of dog, or dogs: although it has just one body, it boasts three heads, all fierce. This pet is the original hellhound, and is one heck of a handful.

Appearance
Cerberus has a hulking, oversized, canine body topped off by three heads, each one crammed full of snarling, snapping teeth. Traditionally, only one head sleeps at a time. Cerberus won't look good on your couch, but will ensure that your porch looks like the entryway to the nearest Hell's Angels frathouse.

Character

In a word: aggressive. But that really shouldn't surprise you. Not only is cerberus the celebrated gatekeeper of Hades, it comes from the most mixed-up family imaginable. It is the son of the hundred-headed giant Typhon and the half-nymph, half-serpent Echidna, and has eight brothers and sisters, all more or less monstrous (the sphinx, the hydra, and the chimera are all siblings). This is one puppy you won't want to breed from, but it's a fabulous guard. Once installed on your driveway, it will spell the end to Girl Scouts bearing cookies, and will give kitchen-equipment salespeople the firm brush-off.

• Cerberus
(Canis Vehementius)

What you need

• **A firm hand and lots of patience.** You can tame cerberus, but it isn't at all easy. You will need to research ancient pet manuals.

• **Quite a lot of money and an excellent local butcher.** All three heads are eternally hungry. Cerberus likes plenty of good, raw meat.

• **A developed musical sense.** Just like everyone else, this hound has a softer side. Despite its savage appearance, Cerberus loves music and can be charmed into quiescence, or even a light doze, with skilled playing. The lyre is its favorite instrument, but the flute and oboe have been known to work, too. Concentrate on the classics: rock does nothing for this hound dog's refined tastes.

• **A kennel with three windows.** An essential item, of course …

Feeding habits

Forget etiquette—cerberus feeding is not a pretty sight. Just lay an animal carcass down in front of it, and all three heads will go into a snapping, snarling feeding frenzy. However, there's another, rather touching, side to its bestial gluttony. Its love of honey cake goes way back, and if you're a keen cook, you can spoil cerberus with freshly baked treats. Snarling brute will turn to slobbering puppy as it lingers over each and every crumb. If you need it to settle down in advance of your mother-in-law's arrival, slip a light sleeping pill into the mix (there's also a precedent for this— your pet's ancestor was once successfully calmed with honey and opium).

Does love grow?
Your baby cerberus will make you go "Aaah," but when fully grown, it's more likely to elicit an "Oh!" or even an "Aaargh!"

Veterinary care

Cerberus may have three heads, but it's all dog, and regular veterinary care is what is needed. Most veterinarians, however, will be nervous of making a house call. Find one with a musical bent, get him or her to play a simple lullaby on the lyre, and your pet won't wake up until after it has had its shots. If your veterinarian isn't musical, and neither of you is willing to take up an instrument, stock up on honey cake.

Rise above
Cerberus isn't the largest pet you could choose, but he is probably one of the more challenging.

Adult height at shoulder: 4' 2".

Companion pets

Who needs companions when you have family around you? Any evening that sees cerberus entertaining the hydra, the chimera, and the sphinx will be lively. The first three tend to tough it out, while the sphinx stays in the corner, sneering, asking riddles, and being the family wiseass. When the growling and hissing cease, dinner can be served. However, you may want to leave the party early—none of these four has cute table manners. Blood is thicker than water …

Fun things to do with your cerberus

• *Play Frisbee—fleet of feet and ahead of the game, cerberus's catching skills are unmatched. Get one made in stainless steel.*

• *Leash up and walk your pet around the toughest neighborhoods— watch the homeboys and their pit bulls scatter as you approach. This isn't big and it isn't clever, but it certainly is good fun.*

• *Join a chamber-music group—watch three ferocious heads nod and six eyelids droop with pleasure as you fiddle your way through one of Schubert's more soulful quartets.*

Gatekeeper of choice for those for whom one dog is not nearly enough.

Dog days
Cerberus is one hell of a guard dog. Once in its kennel at the entrance to your driveway, it will keep visitor levels down.

EXTREME PETS

Only the very brave should consider the pets in this section. They are extreme in size, and have anti-social tendencies that range from seriously elusive to positively vile. There are some that belch fish, others that breathe fire, and some that eat children. This is a danger zone—you have been warned.

How to live with a ...

KRAKEN

*I*f you thought "floating islands" and "pet-keeping" were words that belonged in entirely different manuals, you could be in for a gigantic shock. On a fair number of occasions the impossibly large kraken has been mistaken for an island by unwitting sailors, and its body used as a campsite. Picture a giant squid in your mind, and multiply it a few thousand times. The kraken takes extreme pet-keeping to new heights, and hidden depths.

Character

The kraken hails from northern Scandinavia. It has a rather frightening reputation, but in the right hands this pet can be as enormously rewarding as it is challenging. It spends large chunks of time slumbering on the ocean floor, but also enjoys stretching out, islandlike, on the surface, basking in the sun. If provoked or irritable, it has the wherewithal to encircle vessels and drag them back into the deep, in a swirling, deadly vortex of its own making. This tendency will have to be rigorously restricted or controlled. It may seem like a huge responsibility, but with the right vocation and location, you can handle it.

• Kraken
(Cephalopod Giganticus)

Appearance
The kraken is a gargantuan sea creature, squidlike in its appearance, vast in length, and a mile and a half in width. Its sucker-studded tentacles are as tall as an average ship's mast, conveniently enough, and its eyes are as big as a boat, with pupils as fiery and bright as lighthouses that illuminate the night.

What you need

• A coastal property with a large private water area. The kraken will need room in which to stretch its tentacles and sunbathe, clear of domestic and international shipping lanes or leisure-boat activities.

• Plenty of indigestion tablets and mouthwash. The kraken has an antique digestive system and terrible breath. A belch can bring up a semidigested, foul-smelling seafood banquet, in its own brown coulis.

• A comprehensive public-liability insurance policy. Just in case the Global Positioning System of a yacht or cruise liner fails in the vicinity, you will need to be comprehensively insured against any unfortunate incidents.

• A large "No Camping" sign. Attach it gently to your basking kraken. It will never know.

Tower of strength
The demands of this pet are head and shoulders above the rest. Are you robust enough to share your life, and your home, with it? Think about it.

As a pet, it poses challenges of titanic proportions.

Feeding habits

The kraken's natural diet is made up of plenty of fish, other, much smaller squids, and, on occasion, the odd whale. Interestingly, its name derives from a Norwegian dialect word, *krake*, meaning "sickly animal" or "twisted thing," and the kraken does appear, when provoked, to have an unhealthy appetite for human flesh, or at least that of sailors, perhaps because of the added salt. The kraken has been known to consume an entire ship's crew at one sitting, but taking them off the menu should limit this antisocial tendency. It digests its food for several months, letting out a salty, fish-laden, murky, liquid belch from time to time.

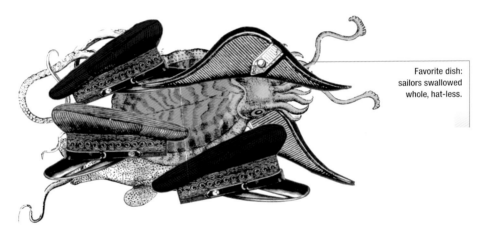

Favorite dish:
sailors swallowed
whole, hat-less.

Veterinary care

However sickly it may get, you won't find it at all easy to recruit someone to attend to a cranky kraken. Marine biologists and veterinarians won't touch it, even with the most sophisticated, squid-proof subaqua equipment, in case they are mistaken for sailors, but they will happily do long-distance consulting. Hands-on care will have to be administered by a third party who has won the kraken's confidence—that's you, by the way. Teuthologists (squid experts) will be fascinated to lay eyes, if not hands, on your pet.

Companion pets

The shortlist of possible candidates brave enough to risk a close friendship includes: the Loch Ness monster, a possible distant relative that doesn't get out much; the Norse sea serpent Jormungard, so large it surrounds the Earth and bites its own tail; and the leviathan, a vast creature that is over 900 miles in length, with seven heads and 300 eyes. They could play shipwrecks and battleships and swap notes on how to display truly monstrous behavior.

Fun things to do with your kraken

- *Set up a theme park and name a roller coaster "The Kraken"—mirror the ups and downs of your own relationship and make everybody scream.*

- *Cause a cartographic sensation—casually drop into a conversation that you have discovered an uncharted island.*

- *Sell fishing rights to your private waterway—schools of fish are drawn to the loud belches of the kraken, making it a great fishing ground for brave fishermen. You make a profit, even if they don't.*

Reel 'em in
The kraken is the biggest bait that you could never get hold of. It reels in the fish, and leaves the fisherman reeling.

How to live with a …

DRAGON

*I*f you wake up one day and think to yourself, "Hey, I'm bored. Maybe I should get a dragon to play with?" go back to sleep. Owning such a fabulous creature without being in the right place at the right time, or in your right mind, could become your worst nightmare. Before you dream of putting dragons on your wish list, grapple with some very big ideas. They are huge, live for centuries, and breathe fire. Getting a dragon is the biggest decision you will ever make.

Character

It isn't just a question of "to be or not to be" a dragon-owner. The choice reads like a takeout menu, but the bill and repercussions are much bigger: Western, Chinese, Indian, earth- or water-based, one head or several, with extra flames, smoke or mist, extremely big, or just very large. Our suggestion for the novice is the Western male dragon (WMD). Originally from Europe, the WMD is now available to owners in North America and some parts of Australasia. A fire-belching, treasure-hoarding, lair-guarding, keen-sighted, instinctively fierce dragon with supersonic hearing, you will come to tame and love it like you would a kitten.

• Dragon
(Draco Inflammabilis)

Appearance
Four-legged, with large hind legs and feet plus smaller front legs. It has one big head (or several) with a long snout, forked tongue, and sharp teeth. It has a long, barbed, coilable tail, wide, membranous, claw-tipped wings, a large scaly body of variable hues, mostly green and yellow, and a dorsal ridge of sharp spines. And it is bigger than your average house.

What you need

• **Monstrous amounts of money, land, and time.** You will need a vast property, complete with hills, mountains, swamps, or rivers for your fully fledged dragon (actually, they carry on growing throughout their lives), a serious budget for feeding, accommodating, and domesticating it, and the dedication of a lifetime (yours, your kids', and your grandkids' …).

• **Just a sign.** Commission a plaque saying *Here be Dragons*. You won't need security alarms, close-circuit cameras, or guard dogs to contain things, as these three little olde-worlde words will keep you and your neighbors safe (from each other …).

• **Drastic measurements.** Just like any other reptile, your dragon will need a well-heated, temperature-controlled environment in which to sleep, digest, and grow. It may breathe fire, but it can still catch a cold.

> *The biggest, hottest pet on the market today.*

Crack it
If you still aren't at all sure which came first—the dragon or the egg—now's your big chance to find out.

Veterinary care

Call your local practice and request a veterinarian specializing in home visits for reptiles. If they ask what size, you may find that you need to be somewhat economical with the truth, or settle for video-conference care. Indigestion and nostril burns are among the most common complaints for a dragon. Gases build up in the dragon's stomach and if not expelled as ignited methane, they can cause internal damage. Your veterinarian will need to be equipped with flame-resistant clothing, an extinguisher, and a degree in chemistry.

Feeding habits

Dragons aren't particularly fussy about what they eat, to be honest. They are omnivores, rather than strict carnivores, although in days of yore, their diet did include large quantities of sheep, cattle, maidens, and knights, plus steeds, armor, and clothing. Your main concern will be size and regularity of portions. Keeping up with its gargantuan appetite will be a culinary and

Relax
End a busy day's dragon-keeping with a nice warm drink. Check it's not piping hot. Your pet's teeth are surprisingly heat-sensitive.

financial challenge. Supplement live-animal-based fare with nuts, berries, fruit, and cereal to vary intake and provide vitamins. It appreciates a bowl of chicken-stock soup before bed as much as the next lair-weary dragon. Join it for a nightcap. If Ness, the lake dragon, comes over, stock up on fish.

Companion pets

Don't invite Nelly around or she may pack her trunk sooner than expected. Dragons don't get on with elephants. It goes way back to when they fought over food, and dragons were known for line rage. Just seeing an elephant might trigger a painful memory. The basilisk is one of the family, but not exactly an easy guest. Their friendship should remain one of correspondence not contact. Have counseling before ordering a Western female dragon.

Fun things to do with your dragon

- *Rent-a-pet—heraldic artists will fight to the death to paint your dragon at life-drawing classes. Offer its services as a model, even pose alongside it so they can create your own coat of arms as payment.*

- *Dragon ride—after proper training, and with its permission, saddle up your dragon and sell tickets to ride.*

- *Dress up as St. George or Georgina—stage a mock battle at a local fund-raising event. Slaughter the other attractions.*

Art for art's sake
Provide large easels and nonflammable paints, and practice regular fire drills.

Important physical feature: hypnotic eyes.

How to live with a …

YETI

Appearance
Imagine the Incredible Hulk with a coat of long, reddish hair, or a mountain gorilla with an unusual inside-leg measurement. Between 7 and 9 feet tall, with fur obscuring much of its face, it has unusually large hands and feet. If you find the larger primates attractive, the yeti will have a special appeal.

*I*f you're a natural recluse, and not fond of excessive in-your-face, one-to-one neediness in your companion, then perhaps you should consider acquiring one of the famously shy members of the bigfoot family. If previous excursions into pet-owning have been limited to clingy little Pomeranians or lap-hugging Chihuahuas, and you're looking for something much more independent, the yeti may bring welcome relief. This is no hands-on pet, it's more of a footloose one, and those feet are very, very big.

• Yeti
(Wereyehteh)

Character
Yeti, sasquatch, yowie, and bigfoot appear to be different names for broadly the same beast, although it's hard to be sure, since one of the many characteristics they share is an intense reluctance to interact with others. "Elusive" best describes this group. The closest you may get to your pet is the occasional glimpse of a huge, furry figure striding through a coppice. You may have to content yourself with viewing its impressive footprints in the mud or snow, which can be up to 20 inches long. Those who have come close to a yeti describe their demeanor as modest and their manner as gentle.

What you need

• **A great deal of land.** A private mountain with plenty of icy wastes for the Tibetan yeti, or a large tract of woodland with lots of dense tree cover, should you favor the North American, Canadian, or Australian branch. Or you could opt for both, if you are a billionaire who values privacy and can afford as much of it as either of you would like.

• **A good camera plus digital-recording system.** Keep a record of sightings (even encounters) with your pet. Otherwise, your friends may refuse to believe it exists, and may mock.

• **A dedication to organic values.** Your pet lives off the land and, albeit hardy, needs to be kept safe from pesticides, organophosphates, and other nasties. You don't want to inadvertently poison your pet.

Free spirit
If you live in a midtown bachelor apartment, you will have to forget the yeti. And it wouldn't be seen dead in a condo.

Rich, reclusive pet-owners need look no further.

Feeding habits

The yeti is the original hunter-gatherer, and lives off the land. It shops very well in its own private open-air market, and always chooses healthy options. You won't ever lay eyes on a yeti in a fast-food outlet or a drive-thru. Your pet is an omnivore: it spends much of its time collecting nuts, berries, grubs, and fruit, and supplements its diet with such small birds and animals as it is able to catch. It is neither gourmet nor gourmand. Ancient Tibetan legends suggest that it has a taste for humans, but no yeti, bigfoot, or sasquatch attacks on humans have been recorded within living memory.

Veterinary care

Veterinarians rarely get to see a yeti. Its healthy eating plan, hardy outdoor life, and marvelous exercise regime constitute an exemplary lifestyle. It could act as a poster boy for the National Association for Heart Health, giving lectures in schools about the benefits of forest-foraging and making your own shelter. Just occasionally, though, it will crack a tooth on a particularly tough nut, thereby needing a talented and calm-mannered dentist. Shy though the yeti is, it's just like the rest of us when it comes to toothache.

Companion pets

Yetis have never been observed in groups, so you may find that your pet is happiest being left to live a solitary life. Should you feel less reclusive from time to time yourself and in need of more companionship, say at Thanksgiving or on other special occasions, you might want to consider inviting another shy, wild lover of solitude: the unicorn. Reconcile yourself to the idea that these beasts are more likely to tolerate one another than to become close friends.

Fun things to do with your yeti

- *Cross-country skiing—its huge feet and natural balance let it glide and slide without skis through thick virgin snow. Follow at a discreet distance using its tracks.*

- *Run foraging courses—"wild-harvested" food is in fashion. Urban children and doting eco-parents will pay quite highly for the privilege of following your yeti, collecting nuts. No cameras.*

- *Learn to yodel—its natural call is a warm, husky yell, not unlike Mongolian throat-singing; if sharing a mountain habitat, perform an energetic duet before breakfast.*

Making tracks
The yeti makes a great snowplow. You will see it with ease on the slopes, but you won't spot it at the après-ski party.

Important physical feature: flat-as-a-plank feet.

How to live with a ...

BUNYIP

*T*he bunyip comes in a variety of sizes, shapes, and colors, and will be delivered direct from the Australian outback. Taking delivery of your pet will be exciting, just like winning a mystery prize, since you can't be sure of what yours will look like until it arrives. If you are somewhat vague and indecisive, if your life is fluid rather than concrete, then you should consider this shapeshifting companion, with its indefinite appearance and ambiguous profile. If the question of certainty is not a priority, a bunyip could be the answer.

Appearance

Most bunyips look like seals, with flippers, tusks, and a horse's tail. Some are scaly like a crocodile, others are available from the fur or feathered range. There is also a hairy, shaggy-dog model. Some sport long necks, others, short; a few have long arms and claws, others have horns. Life's a lottery; so is bunyip-keeping.

Character

Its name comes from an Australian Aboriginal word meaning "devil" or "spirit" and it is much talked of in ancient Dreamtime stories. The bunyip is amphibious. It lives in creeks, lakes, swamps, and billabongs, and takes its job as guardian of water holes deeply seriously, defending its damp patch with vim and vigor, and bellowing loudly and terrifyingly if approached. It will treat intruders with rigorous malevolence, and has a penchant for women and children, whom it finds easier to deal with, if not drag down, drown, and devour. Having said that, it's an interesting and useful pet—an enigma with tusks. And it can't half yell.

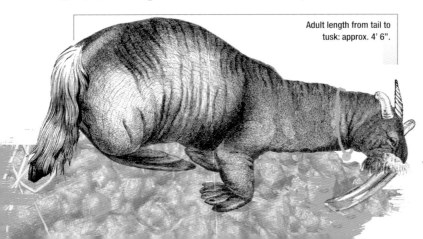

Adult length from tail to tusk: approx. 4' 6".

• Bunyip
(Bunyipus Molestus)

What you need

• **A property with a moat or lake.** All bunyips make highly effective security guards when defending their watery territory. Ensure there is a creek, lake, or moat in front of your house, and it will issue an earsplitting cry should an intruder try to enter without permission—beware the hound of the billabong. If your home is your castle, then your bunyip's is the moat, and you won't need a doorbell.

• **Safe accommodation for little 'uns.** Keep your baby bunyip indoors at first. If it is stolen, or kidnapped, its mother, wherever she is, will let out a fearful howl, and will flood all the nearby homes, even those perched high on hills, in order to flush out the lost bunyip. Any human touched by the water will become a black swan.

Swanning around
It's right up there with the cerberus as fabulous guard.

> *If it's history and mystery you want (with a bit of bite), you won't look back.*

Feeding habits

The bunyip can't get enough of freshwater crayfish, known down under as "yabbies." They should be raw, fresh, and self-caught, so you don't need to be good at fishing or cooking to satisfy your pet. However, always ensure there is a plentiful supply of claws, fresh-frozen if necessary, otherwise your pet could be tempted by larger sources of protein, carbohydrates, and fatty deposits to satisfy its appetite—women and children first, of course. It would probably enjoy a lobster on its birthday, if your budget permits. This is not an expensive pet, but it could cost you some friends if they pop around unannounced.

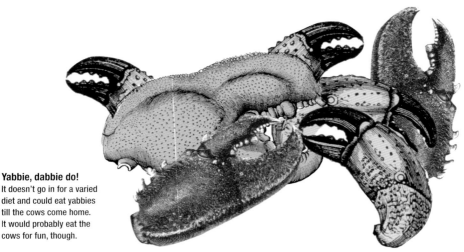

Yabbie, dabbie do!
It doesn't go in for a varied diet and could eat yabbies till the cows come home. It would probably eat the cows for fun, though.

Veterinary care

The bunyip is usually of robust, if not rude, health, given its largely sensible diet rich in fish oils, and the fact that it keeps itself both busy and active, spending much of its evening threshing the water. Intended as a deterrent to all who might dare to approach, this activity is also a useful form of aerobic exercise. In the event of a vital visit by a veterinarian, ensure a male practitioner comes armed with freshwater crustaceans to appease his patient, and ear plugs to spare his ears.

Companion pets

It doesn't really do friends. As a water-hole-ic, it has few hobbies outside its 24/7 job. Once you have bonded with your bunyip, you will be its only true friend—its instinct is to view other humans as a meal ticket. A night owl by nature, any socializing takes place in the darker hours. It might fancy dinner by a pool with a mermaid, followed by a midnight swim, but she might be dinner, and it would swim alone.

A loner
Too busy guarding water-holes, it won't make many friends on dry land. Their reputation as child eaters limits the number of party invitations received.

Fun things to do with your bunyip

- *Buy a hot tub—ask it to join you and get it to splash around with its flippers and tail. It will soon become a lovely, bubbly Jacuzzi.*

- *Join a local all-female choir—you will soon be singing solo.*

- *Relocate to a coastal location—offer the services of your bunyip as a life-endangering foghorn.*

- *Have fun at Halloween—put up a sign encouraging trick-or-treating by noisy local children. You will need to do it only once.*

How to live with a ...

HYDRA

$\mathcal{H}$ydra of Lerna sounds a somewhat grand name for a pet, and it certainly has an unusual pedigree. In Grecian days gone by, the first hydra was sired by the many-dragon-headed and multiserpent-limbed Typhon, and by Echidna, who had her own challenges as half beautiful woman and half, significantly less seductive, serpent. Its pet ID should carry its full name Lernaian Hydra, Water Serpent, and the wide-angled photograph will reveal a fine head upon sloping shoulders; nine heads in total, to be precise, and all of them in your care.

Appearance
Nine separate, and yet co-dependent, snake heads, long-necked and tongued, sit proudly, and, it must be said, quite menacingly, upon a huge, scaly, twisting, sometimes writhing, serpent's body. The central head is immortal, everlasting, never stumped for an answer or a plan for the future. The remaining eight can double their chances with ease.

Character

The hydra hails from Mycenae, Greece, where it would spend its time enjoying life as a multiheaded marshland serpent. Innate ancient instincts might provoke it to venture out on frenzied flock-frightening, land-ruining, villager-munching raids. These will need curtailing, if not cauterizing, but certainly not in the brutal fashion practiced upon its ancestors. If a hydra loses a head, two will replace it. Ancient manuals illustrate the now banned practice of stump-scorching as prevention against multiple regrowth, an early, savage form of electrolysis. Many wounded hydras languished in rescue shelters in antiquity.

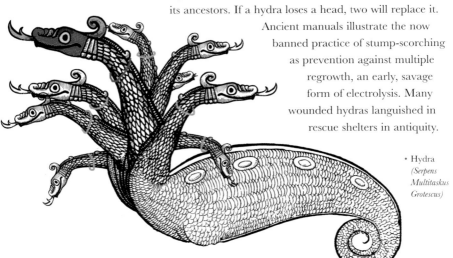

• Hydra
(Serpens
Multitaskus
Grotescus)

What you need

• **Industrial quantities of industrial-strength breath freshener.**
The hydra's hyperhalitosis defies description, except to say it can poison
water, turn fields brown, and the face of anyone in the near—and far—
vicinity a swampy-water green. If breaths could kill, its breath would.

• **A lakeside, river, or sea-front property.** The hydra will need
a watery playground in which to unwind, located at a safe distance from
appropriate, custom-built, well-secured, half-door stabling, accommodating
its high headcount housing needs and Houdini-like ability to escape it.

• **Time and patience.** Your pet will need quality face time with you as
its owner, and nine one-on-one counseling sessions to get its heads around
any concerns. Two (or in this case, ten) heads are better than one.

Multitasking
Don't lose your head
while all around the
hydra is keeping its
nine. Commission a
fashionable, yet secure,
high-rise hydra home.

Feeding habits

The hydra is a keen carnivore. It doesn't give small prey a second thought, preferring a larger-sized takeout, such as a sheep or cow. Given that nine mouths feed just one stomach, indigestion is an issue, particularly when the heads don't share their meal. Try introducing regular fasting days. In order to speed up digestion, the hydra, like other snakes, will head home for a warm snooze. Keep the heating at a steady 86°F. If temperatures fall below 50°F it will regurgitate its food, and clearing up nine half-digested sheep is no picnic. Dining out is not an option—the cost per head is far too great.

Veterinary care

Should your hydra have difficulty keeping its head above water, hire a veterinarian who specializes in reptiles and exotic pets. He or she will need to multitask, have no sense of smell, or a very powerful mask, and demonstrate a talent for math. Large snakes are usually treated in pairs, in a "buddy system," but the long division just doesn't work for your hydra, unless the immortal head is treated as a separate entity. You will need to take advice on this. Math can stink at times.

Companion pets

The hydra's heads should never feel lonely or want for company, but if the nine heads ever quarrel, you could consider inviting some of the hydra's unusual relatives over. Ask three three-headed cerberi over for some rewarding one-to-one time, and possibly rowdy play. The hydra's ancient friend is the sea crab, which tried to help out during a stump-scorching attempt in antiquity. An odd couple, but they go way back.

The Houdini-like pet with halitosis.

Fun things to do with your hydra

- *Go fishing—with your hydra at your side, you can't fail, although it might reduce your catch by swallowing a few. Spare the rod, your pet is in it for the long haul.*

- *Make money at charity events—people will throw money at its nine Aunt Sally heads. It can catch it in its mouths, and pass it on to you … eventually.*

- *Get it to pretend to be a hat stand—watch your mother-in-law faint when her new bonnet moves …*

Heads or tails
Well, they do say, "Get a hat, get ahead …" Hydras can be very useful to have around the home.

Important physical feature: nine in- and co-dependent heads.

How to live with a ...

CHIMERA

*I*f your ideal pet is still not picture-perfect in your mind, pick up a pencil, close your eyes, and draw. And if you can't make head nor tail of the result, you may well have come up with the chimera. This lion-goat-serpent mix certainly looks like one of nature's doodles at the end of a long day at the drawing board. It's an extreme hybrid, like a furry, hairy, scaly, three-way conversation. It can't talk, but it spouts fire, so you will soon get the message.

Character

Its name comes from the Greek for she-goat, *khimaira*. It has intrigued veterinarians and poets since the 8th century BCE, when the Greek poet Homer first waxed lyrical about its leonine, serpentine, and, he thought, divine properties. It is the heterogeneous product of the union of Typhon and Echidna, and spent time terrorizing the folk of Lycia, now Turkey. Bodily eruptions are its forte—not content with having a lion's head, it grew a snake's and a goat's. Swift and strong, its ancestors harried cattle and devoured humans. It is no slouch today.

Appearance
Pet portrait-painters could make an interesting, if expensive, triptych of the chimera, with its lion's foreparts and legs, goat's belly and head, and serpent's tail, with mouth to match. Pretty as a picture it isn't, but what it lacks in symmetry, it makes up for in diversity.

• Chimera
(Chimaera Confusus)

What you need

• **A large supply of fire extinguishers.** It can vomit fire from each of its heads when roused, so be prepared for eruptions. Avoid being inflammatory in its multiearshot. If the snake or lion lose their cool, you could burn your goat.

• **A comprehensive knowledge of astrology.** When attempting to understand your pet's character, remember it is a Leonine Capricorn, born in the year of the snake. Leos take this stuff seriously, so don't affront it by playing the goat (or taking the hiss.)

• **An awareness of its growing needs.** When your chimera first arrives as a cub-kid-hatchling you will have a three-in-one baby to feed, but conjoined and multi-species. It will stretch your parenting skills to the max.

> *For those who agree that three heads are better than one.*

Paws for thought
The child chimera has a certain charm that decreases in intensity as it increases in size. Make sure you never get on its baby goat.

Feeding habits

Pet manuals translated from the Greek suggest the chimera used to indulge in some "slash and burn" antics, terrorizing, grilling, and then devouring all in its path, humans included. Some of these tales may be apocryphal or hard to stomach, but what isn't lost in translation is your responsibility to get the idea of a more balanced carnivorous and herbivorous diet, with fewer lawsuits, into its heads. You will need plenty of land for grazing and hunting, but ensure you have a well-stocked freezer for emergencies. Remember, you have three extra mouths to feed now. It can defrost its own food with ease, and is a blowtorch par excellence for your crème brûlées.

Veterinary care

Three veterinarians for three pets mean three bills for three ills. This will account for the lion's share of your expenditure on your pet, but do bear it in mind when you are deciding if your budget can stretch to the chimera. Alternatively, look for a veterinarian who has got a bachelor's degree in reptiles, a masters in farm animals, and a doctorate in big game. With all that experience, he or she may not come cheap. It might be wise to suggest a layer of fireproof clothing to avoid third-degree burns.

Fun things to do with your chimera

- *Get it a job at the meteorological office—its appearance was thought to predict storms and volcanoes. Will the staff weather it?*

- *Go camping with your chimera—get it to light a fire, boil the water, and do some toast the next morning. Who needs a gas ring?*

- *Send a photo of your pet to* National Geographic *magazine—all the genetic scientists in town will be on the phone offering millions.*

Companion pets

Its siblings include the dogged cerberus, serpentine hydra, and enigmatic sphinx. This is a family of strong characters and big egos. Family reunions will be memorable, but beware fireworks. Parties, and guest lists, should be closely monitored. Never invite pegasus: in days of very old, they exchanged fiery words. Get your guests to come as they are—who needs fancy dress when you look like a hydra? Make sure, though, that you do a head count at the end of the soiree.

Important physical feature: more than the average number of heads.

Party animals
You can imagine what fun a chimera family reunion can be.

How to live with an ...

OGRE

Appearance
Huge, hirsute, helplessly muscle-bound, and often hairy-bearded, sometimes horned, it has large, ugly feet and hands, and an oversized, frightening head. The only small organ is its brain. Its tusklike teeth are unspeakable, its skin is gray to green and all hues between, and it has zero fashion sense. It's big, it isn't clever, but it's all yours.

*T*his is a double no-brainer: the choice and the pet. The ogre is a great big humanoid hunk o' muscle and bone, but it's mind-bendingly low on gray matter. If you have a soft spot for the underendowed, aren't expecting to be stretched intellectually by your companion, and want to give a jolly gray giant a home, then go for it. The pet store will welcome you with open arms, although saying goodbye to the ogre will leave a big hole behind.

• Ogre
(Orcus Maximus)

Character
The ogre's name derives from the Latin *orcus*, meaning "realm of the dead," "god of Hades," or "monster of the underworld." None of these descriptions are overly endearing, but words won't break your bones. Talking of which, pet-lore manuals show images of your companion sporting sticks, stones, clubs, axs, and cudgels, but you will be able to wean it off these with a well-judged mix of love, cunning, and training. The ogre is instinctively cruel, but also shy, if not a little cowardly, and easily outwitted. All it really needs is stability and a big hug. By the way, it's a shapeshifting cannibal, too ...

What you need

• **Palatial accommodation with a large basement.** Ancient pet manuals place ogres in castles and palaces. They spend large periods of time underground—presumably due to a mix of natural shyness and stupidity. Get your pet to help you construct an appropriately sized home. Who needs earth-digging equipment and scaffolding when you have the biggest builder in town? Issue instructions slowly, repeatedly, and with pictures.

• **Extraordinary sleeping arrangements.** Forget the great big bed in the three bears' cottage, the ogre needs one as large as a house.

• **Teaching experience.** Get professionally trained. Installing even rudimentary information into the pea-size brain of the ogre may be too great a task for the amateur. And you will need to get a few concepts across, among them: "Don't eat your owner."

DIY
The ogre is ideal if you fancy a self-build home without huge labor costs. Your brain, its brawn—a perfect construction.

A pet that will eat the heart out of your neighbors.

Feeding habits

The ogre has cannibal tendencies, or so the story goes. It likes the tender flesh of children, but if ever permitted to shop for itself, it will always down adult-sized portions. However, fear not: you will be able to dupe your pet with ease and a little culinary cunning and knowledge. All you have to do is fake the food.
Serve lip-smacking, tenderized steak tartare in the shape of a young child, or make crepes suzette and pretend they are the carpaccio-thin slices of a young French girl. Return triumphantly from the market with a fresh delivery of tilapia. Serve a Tom Collins on its birthday ... No kidding.

Veterinary care

You should consult a doctor keen to climb the career ladder and happy to bring his or her own, along with supersized instruments, to tend to your sickly ogre. He or she will need to multiply drug dosages to cope with the extra body mass of your ogre. Buy shampoo, shaving cream, antiperspirant, and other toiletries in bulk for your hygiene-shy hulk. Barbers and podiatrists will charge extra, given their increased workload. Dentists will need industrial machinery. Psychiatrists and brain surgeons won't have much to work on, so save money on their fees.

Companion pets

Sadly, it won't make friends easily, due to introversion, a general lack of conversation, and a shortage of interests. It will dwarf other humanoids with the size of its physique, if not its intellect. If your property and means can accommodate the consequences, introduce it to an ogress. Just as large and physically unappealing, the female is much friendlier, if equally challenged. You will hear the thud-thud of big ogre feet in no time ...

Fun things to do with your ogre

- *Get a leg up—get a great view of the game by sitting on your pet's shoulders. Who's going to complain?*

- *Shift-scared—read fairy tales to your pet at night and remind it how its ancestors turned into scary lions. Watch your horrid stepmother's jaw drop when it enters her bedroom …*

- *Role-play—female owners should join the local amateur dramatic society and propose a stage performance of* Beauty and the Beast *or* Shrek. *You're both made for the part.*

- *Donate ogre organs—with no harm to itself and considerable advantage to any number of others, it could donate an organ, for example, a kidney. Not the brain, of course, not even to science.*

Keep it in the family
If you want a large family, find an ogress for your pet. Think big—very, very big. Extended doesn't even begin to cover it.

Length of baby at birth: 1' 9".

PART-HUMAN
COMPANIONS

If you fancy pet-keeping with a human touch, this is the chapter for you. Man-horse, man-bull, man-goat, man-lion, girl-fish, girl-seal, girl-snake, girl-lion, or just plain fairy: all of the human hybrids are here.

How to live with a ...

CENTAUR

*I*f you'd rather watch the game on television than go to the opera, if you love a laugh, and are always up for a rowdy night with your pals, a centaur may prove a most compatible companion. It is important not to be fooled by its elegant and impressive looks. Known by its most ardent admirers as "uncomplicated," this half-man, half-horse has been much more harshly described by those less enamored of its tendencies. Only you can know if this is the pet for you.

Character

Greatly celebrated in modern pet manuals as wise and measured, its reputation comes from just one notable ancestor, Chiron. Tutor to the Greek heroes Theseus and Achilles, Chiron was calm, knowledgeable, and kind, but even centaur fans agree he was the exception to the rule. The bloodline of the majority of centaurs can be traced back to Ixion, one of the more rackety kings of Thessaly, and Nephele, a cloud nymph. Mix a licentious aristocrat with something as ephemeral and formless as a cloud, and you get an energetic party animal with little impulse control. A centaur is an unsuitable pet for the fainthearted.

Appearance

A well-toned, attractive, male torso, equipped with a rippling six-pack, melds just below the waist into the sleek body of a horse, complete with two pairs of equine legs and a tail. Most centaurs have quite a handsome head, often liberally bearded, and noble, classical profiles. There are no she-centaurs. This is a classic handsome pet.

• Centaur
(Centaurus Challengus)

What you need

• **A large private estate.** Impractical as an urban pet, the centaur's natural habitat is woodland with grassy glades. The human part needs covered accommodation—a good-size stable with cable access is best. It will need plentiful supplies of junk television and mindless computer games. If bored, it can become destructive.

• **A love of sport.** Centaurs are gregarious and sporting, so ask some of its friends around, and yours, to watch the game. Suggest a spot of fast, aggressive soccer or touch football. Sagittarius, the Archer centaur, had excellent aim, so an archery contest could hit the spot.

• **A relaxed personality.** If you're a poet, philosopher, or possess other rarefied interests, the centaur is really not for you. Try a phoenix or a mermaid instead.

> *A fun-loving hellraiser in a deceptively sleek and sophisticated package.*

Don't junk the TV
"Centaur in the City" won't be a new hit, but provide your pet with constant television access or else view signals of unrest.

Feeding habits

The feeding needs of the centaur should cause you less concern than its drinking habits. However, its twin stomachs, human and equine, make dual demands on the nutritional front (and back), and you will need some decent grazing and a well-stocked larder. Otherwise, the diet is straightforward. On the drinking side, you need to be very careful. Even half a glass of low-alcohol beer will affect a centaur. It is very susceptible and unable to hold its liquor. If it has more than a drop, you could be looking at redecorating. A drunken man attached to an out-of-control horse spells domestic disaster. It gets very lightheaded and weaklegged, and drinker's droop is only one of its problems. You will need to kick ass or clean up its act.

Veterinary care

Employ a reliable doctor upfront, and an experienced equine veterinarian can bring up the rear, but you need to warn both that home visits will be a prerequisite—a centaur is happy to go to the doctor, but will kick up a fuss in the reception area. Centaurs have dual sets of digestive organs, so the halves can be treated independently. The double liver can be useful in helping your centaur cope with the physical side effects of its drinking.

Companion pets

The satyr is a possible companion (some ancient pet manuals claim the two are distantly related). Both are uninhibited and both have problems holding their drink, making sleepovers dangerous unless they take place in a well-proofed storm cellar. Don't even think about a unicorn as a friend. They may share equine qualities, but the similarity ends there. The unicorn is far too delicate a companion for your protégé.

Fun things to do with your centaur

- *Manage a polo team—form an all-centaur team. There is no sight more impressive than four centaurs, polo sticks in hand, thundering down the field.*

- *Start a bachelor-party company—with the centaur as star performer, results will be consistently and riotously successful. Don't tell the satyr.*

- *Get it a job as a fruit-picker—the height of your centaur, combined with its manual dexterity, will make it an expert in picking even delicate fruit, such as peaches, without bruising. Make sure nobody takes it for a ride.*

Apple of your eye
It makes a handsome and highly efficient apple-plucker. But don't saddle it with too many jobs or else it will kick up a fuss.

**Average height from hoof to hat: 6' 1"
(+ 2 hands).**

How to live with a ...

MERMAID

*I*f you love the ocean, have a fascination for underwater
life, a keen appreciation of female beauty, and can also enjoy
the sight of a handsome tail when you see one, then the
mariner's Miss Universe may prove your ideal companion.
If you're thinking of acquiring a mermaid, however, please
remember that she is so much more than an unusually
enticing poolside ornament. Don't let her overwhelmingly
decorative appearance fool you—mermaids are smart, and
they can be quite demanding, too.

Character

Mermaids are complex and sometimes capricious. Traditionally, seafarers
considered them unlucky (you probably wouldn't want to upset your crew
by inviting one on your yacht for the day), but largely because of their
unusual beauty. A sailor with his eyes on a topless girl won't have them on
the horizon or the wheel. The mermaid can be quite girly—she loves glittery
things and spends hours combing her hair while singing the latest hits to
herself—but she can also be as moody as a teenager. One mermaid captured
by a Dutch ship in the 17th century CE
refused to speak for thirty days before
making her escape.

Appearance

The mermaid takes the
form of a truly lovely girl
from the top of her pretty
head to her slim waist, via
a naked, womanly torso,
and that of a somewhat
overlarge fish below.
Many seafarers have been
seduced by her watery
beauty, her gleaming head
of hair, and even by her
glistening, scaly tail.

• Mermaid
(Serra Terra)

What you need

• **A large lake or, at least, a sizable outdoor pool.** A domesticated mermaid will not enjoy being a big fish in a small pond. And she won't put up with living in a bathtub, so don't even consider it.

• **Plenty of social time and sensitivity.** Mermaids are fun-loving, mischievous, and melancholic by turns, and don't like to spend endless time alone. There is no better companion than a mermaid on top form.

• **Hair-grooming equipment and lots of mirrors.** Whether your mermaid is blonde, brunette or greenhead, obsessive hair-combing forms a large part of her daily routine. Treat her to a three-way mirror and some battery-powered curling tongs. Some owners go all the way and install underwater Hollywood-style mirrors and lighting.

Poolside delight
Enjoy a few cocktails with your tailed companion, but don't give it too many or it may get legless.

The all-singing, all-swimming belle of the marine beauty pageant.

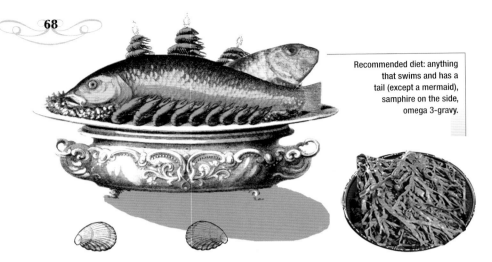

Recommended diet: anything that swims and has a tail (except a mermaid), samphire on the side, omega 3-gravy.

Feeding habits

Your mermaid will enjoy fish, fish, and then more fish, plus a wide range of shellfish, and the occasional side dish of seaweed to keep up her intake of greens. If you're a sashimi lover, you can dine together, but she does not enjoy cooked food and won't touch the tempura. Don't forget, she will most enjoy catching her own supplies; it is possible to keep a mermaid entirely on purchases from your local fish counter, but advisable to offer her at least an occasional opportunity to hone her natural hunting skills. You could always go fishing together.

Veterinary care

With frequent exercise and a diet naturally rich in omega 3 and spirulina, you can expect your mermaid to enjoy fine physical health. However, coping with her mood swings and somewhat sadistic streak (the stuff of mariners' legends since way back) can be demanding. On a bad day, mermaids can display wanton cruelty and depressive tendencies. An understanding veterinarian with a marine-psychology speciality may be your best friend when things get particularly rocky. She will also need regular supplies of hair conditioner and body moisturizer.

Fun things to do with your mermaid

- *Swim laps—your mermaid will be a tireless exercise companion, and should improve your fitness level dramatically.*

- *Form a synchronized-swimming team—the coaching skills of a mermaid are unbeatable. Her underwater grace is legendary, and you will learn to spring from the water with the same glistening smile.*

- *Scuba diving—your mermaid won't need the kit, and she'll take you straight to the most interesting spots, or best pearls, at any dive site.*

- *Hold a karaoke pool party—your mermaid can learn all the latest hits and entertain your guests.*

Companion pets

Mermaids get along well with most sea creatures; their playful personalities mean that dolphins, porpoises, seals, and even small sharks are likely to be greeted with genuine pleasure. Avoid really fierce creatures of the deep, though, in particular the kraken. Of course, you could adopt a sorority of mermaids and become the envy of your male neighbors, or introduce a merman to the mix, at the risk of losing her undivided attention, of course.

Joined at the hip
Enter a local aqua-ballet contest. You will win hands down. Heads, you pick up a trophy; tails, she does.

How to live with a ...

SPHINX

If you opt out of the obvious, enjoy the enigmatic, have a penchant for the puzzling, and don't mind a bit of pouting and posturing, then the sphinx might just be the pet for you. Not only does it have an impeccable classical pedigree, but it also poses an intriguing challenge to its owner. Don't be deceived by the sophisticated appearance—hiding within is an adolescent sensibility with all the in-built insecurities and contradictions. It may exasperate and infuriate, but it will certainly always captivate.

Appearance

A streamlined lion's body, complete with legs, is topped by a glamorous female's upper torso and head, and finished off with a pair of eagle's wings. It sports the must-have accessory of every leonine lady: a long and elegant serpent tail. It evidently didn't inherit its refined appearance from its very unattractive, multidragon-headed father, Typhon.

Character

On a bad day, dealing with this complex pet can feel a bit like taking on the world's most competitive twelve-year-old at Monopoly. Games and puzzles are its specialties. It will never tire of asking you riddles and setting you conundrums, but should you have the temerity to get even a single answer right, it will perform the most extreme act of sulking possible—rushing off and killing itself. Literally. Inside that adult-looking exterior is an insecure teenager just dying for your attention. It's all just "me, me, me" with the sphinx. If it's all "you, you, you," too, think again.

• Sphinx
(Phix Answeri)

What you need

• **An enjoyment of games, but no hunger to win.** Trivial Pursuit®, the toughest crosswords, even the more cerebral card games, all are meat and drink to your pet, but you must be able both to enjoy taking part, and to watch it win. Repeatedly … ad nauseam.

• **Patience, tolerance, and a lack of omniscience.** Make sure you give your demanding housemate plenty of one-to-one time.

• **Space for your sphinx to get a thorough workout.** Its chosen form of exercise is running, and you will find that a well-exercised sphinx is a more placid sphinx. Just as for the rest of us, a lengthy daily run helps to keep her more violent impulses and wilder mood swings in check.

Under the smooth skin and shiny pelt lurks the world's worst loser—bar none.

Room to move
It will put you through your intellectual paces. Ensure it has space for exhausting physical workouts. Enjoy the brief interlude.

Feeding habits

As befits its physique, the sphinx eats in part like a person, and in part like a lion. It's the leonine side of things that you need to keep an eye on. While its human diet may be relatively dainty (and include salad and vegetables), her back end is all carnivore, in claw if not tooth. You should bear in mind that in the event of someone giving the incorrect answer to one of her infernal riddles, it is prone to strangle and then devour them, making mealtimes more than a little fraught, particularly for lesser-brained guests. Try distracting your sphinx during dinner with the *New York Times* crossword.

Veterinary care

As with many mixed-species pets, you need a veterinarian for the back half and a doctor for the front. The wings are mostly for show, as sphinxes prefer running to flying. Just don't let it get competitive with either practitioner. Suggest to any medical attendant that they ask her to open wide and say "Aaah" for the duration of the examination, putting an end to any impromptu quizzes, and ensuring that all parties survive.

Companion pets

The sphinx has plenty of family, but may get more pleasure from the company of a carefully chosen, complementary pet. The satyr will more than match her for sheer immaturity and self-obsession ("You think *you've* got problems? My existential despair far outstrips your rampant libido!"), while a mermaid may make an appropriate friend for her more wayward moods. Play dates should be monitored for explosive losses of temper or childish fallings-out.

Fun things to do with your sphinx

- *Attend a quiz night—whether at your local bar's charity night or a high-school special, it will perform outstandingly.*

- *Start a book group with young, smart, alienated people—chosen texts could include* The Catcher in the Rye, The Outsider, *and perhaps some Nietzsche. Your sphinx will be in her element as you struggle to analyze the complex lives and philosophy of fictional characters …*

- *Encourage your pet to take an on-line degree—keep her restless mind active; not all answers are set in stone.*

Book time together
Enjoy mornings of mutual mental stimulation. The more your sphinx reads, the less it asks. Ensure you do it by the book.

Distinguishing feature: bookish, know-it-all temperament.

How to live with a ...

MINOTAUR

$\mathcal{D}$escribing the minotaur requires some straight-talking. Let's take it from the top. It has the head and neck of a bull and the body of a man. Keeping a minotaur will be a test of your strength, determination, and understanding. It can be bovine, naturally; beastly, instinctively; and bipolar, unfortunately. Unsure if it is man or beast, it struggles with its identity. Owning this pet will be character-building. If you have the hide for it, a minotaur can be very rewarding.

Character

The first minotaur didn't have the best start in life, way back in Ancient Greece. It was the not very lovely and only half-child, love-child of Pasiphae, Queen of Crete, and a white bull. Her infatuation was contrived by Poseidon, god of the sea, in revenge for the refusal of the queen's husband, Minos, son of Zeus, to sacrifice the said bull. The minotaur, "bull of Minos," was a product of a match made in heaven, but looks quite the opposite. It has both a split body and split personality, and is not quite sure which way is up. Fierce, strong, understandably angry, it has cannibal tendencies.

Appearance

The head and neck of a bull, complete with ears, horns, and a full set of pretty savage teeth, sit on the shoulders and muscular body of a man. The spots on its skin have been diagnosed variously as simple rough patches or star marks, linking it to Taurus, the Bull of the zodiac.

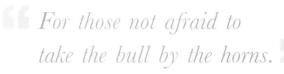

For those not afraid to take the bull by the horns.

Rock-a-bye-baby
A bull-baby in an heirloom bassinet is a rare sight. Your hand could rock the cradle of the only mini-minotaur in town.

What you need

• **A nursery.** The half-calf baby will need a robust cradle when young. Make it as attractive as construction will allow; if you treat it like a human from the start, it may just behave like one. Keep the hood of the stroller firmly up if visiting elderly relatives.

• **A stable environment.** The adult minotaur will need a bachelor pad with creature comforts, in an appropriately agricultural environment.

• **A labyrinth.** Its predecessor lived in a huge maze, where it would lie in wait for an annual treat of seven male youths and seven virgins from Athens. It didn't play with its food, it just gobbled it. Provide the maze to make it feel at home. Take the men and maidens off the menu and mentor your minotaur in manners.

Playing the field
Give it some headroom. If you are buying a downtown apartment, don't get a minotaur. Give your pet a home, but room to roam.

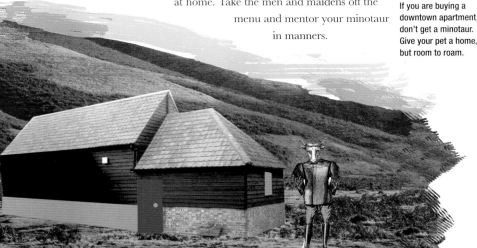

Feeding habits

Historically, the minotaur enjoys Greek food, and in particular that of Athens, but its taste for fourteen human takeouts, albeit only once a year, needs to be stopped in its tracks. You may want to consider employing a team of professionals, including a psychiatrist, a psychonutritionist, or even a hypnotist, in order to help your pet get in touch with its inner part-herbivore, part-omnivore, and give its cannibalistic inclinations the chop, finally. Once the minotaur realizes that it can happily enjoy a varied and tasty diet of Mediterranean food, including even a mezze of fourteen vegetarian and meat-based dishes, it should soon put the annual human banquet to the back of its mind.

• Minotaur
*(Minotauros
Kebabos)*

Veterinary care

Avail yourself of a farm veterinarian and a local doctor to care for the dual physical needs of your minotaur. A regular top-to-toe examination is a good idea and will ensure both parts are working in harmony. It will need daily exercise to keep it in shape, and frequent baths. You might like to treat it to the odd neck massage, bearing in mind the weight it carries on its shoulders. Keep your head and resist any demands for radical cosmetic surgery from your minotaur.

Bull's eye to eye
Let your pet get to know other bovinely inclined folk. Too much wine, and things might decline.

Companion pets

Your minotaur might feel more complete if it developed a friendship with the Babylonian man-bull, sometimes known as the lamassu, which has a crowned man's head on a winged bull's body. It could fly over for a get-together from time to time, and they could exchange views on the pros and cons of being a hybrid, swap unwanted gifts and clothes, play heads or tails, or just talk complete bull.

Key skill: ability to talk the hind legs off a lamassu.

Bullish
Your pet enjoys plenty of face time with other mixed-up folks. Let it get a weight off its mind.

Fun things to do with your minotaur

- *Submit your minotaur's resumé for a job in a local kitchenware store—when it fails the interview, threaten to sue for discrimination against bulls in china shops.*

- *Travel to Pamplona, Spain—take part in the famous bull-running event. The bulls and the runners won't know which way to turn. Olé.*

- *Teach your minotaur to drive the tractor on your farm to round up cattle—it will be head and shoulders above the rest of your workers.*

How to live with a …

SATYR

Satyr-keeping is just like living with a teenager. It gets drunk, enjoys dirty dancing, behaves badly, and if you could make it sleep in a room, it wouldn't tidy it. The satyr's big daddy is Silenus, a prolific father, with a horse's ears, tail, beer belly, and bald head. He enjoyed several liaisons with nymphs and attended, devotedly, the god of wine, Dionysus. Silenus's sons, the satyrs, inherited his penchant for wild parties, dedication to drunkenness, and his unfortunate build. You have been warned.

Appearance
The strong, muscular, hirsute upper body of a man and the lower body of a fairly standard goat are joined at the hip. It has a thick tail, curly hair, full beard, large, pointed ears, and alert eyes. Bony nubs grow to fully-fledged horns as the satyr grows from baby-kid to man-goat.

• Satyr
(Satyrus Invinoveritas)

" The lush
Lothario
of the pet
world. "

Character

"Wine, girls, and loud music." If it could be bothered to write a resumé, these would be the satyr's main interests and hobbies. Lecherous, lazy, licentious, and lustful just about sum it up. Originally from the eastern, mountainous regions of India, it's no 9 to 5 type, but outdoorsy, preferring to hang out in the woods and hills, with their better nymph-ambushing opportunities. It loves playing jokes and pranks, being rude and lewd, but can be very entertaining. It is easily scared, so you should be able to make it toe the line or keep it on the back foot if things get out of hand.

What you need

• **A local drama club.** A chorus of satyrs used to perform at the end of Athenian tragic plays in Ancient Greece, bringing a spot of welcome, if rather ludicrous, light relief. If your pet lets off steam on stage, it could help you both dramatically. Don't let it attend the after-show party.

• **A locked wine and liquor cabinet.** Left to its own devices, a satyr will drink you dry. It has no in-built spirit level, and you will have to take independent measures. Lock up your drinks cabinet or put a big padlock on your wine cellar. Don't take its drinking lying down.

• **A frank talk about sex.** Unless you want a flock of grandkids, you will need to explain to your satyr about the birds, bees, and baby goats.

Feeding habits

The satyr is not that interested in nourishment of a nonliquid kind, and tends to eat on the hoof. As half-goat, it is partly vegetarian; as immature half-man, it likes fast food. When a baby, it should be fed on bottled goat's milk, but toddlers enjoy a normal kid's diet. When out and about in the countryside as an adolescent and "mature" adult, it is happy to forage for its own fast food. However, do try to socialize your pet and teach it some table manners. Insist on dining together or en famille at least one evening a week. Throw a goat-cheese fondue party and invite some friends.

Leg up
Try to recruit a veterinarian prepared to give your pet a man-to-man talk about its less than upright behavior.

Veterinary care

Employ a male veterinarian to handle your pet. He can reinforce the safe-sex message, put in place precautionary measures, and casually mention docking and castrating in a nonthreatening manner. He might even enjoy learning more about what makes a satyr tick (or hic), while advising against excessive alcohol intake, although it may fall on deaf, pointed ears. He will have to trim the satyr's hooves and check for foot rot, but since the satyr spends so much time on its back, this should pose no problem.

Companion pets

Due to its father's unique and extraordinary fertility, the satyr has many brothers, but no sisters, making family reunions large, noisy, macho affairs. You might want to have its siblings over in small groups. The satyr loves nymphs, of course, but is unlikely to go steady with any particular one. It should enjoy the odd get-together with its distant relative and fellow hybrid, the centaur, but after a few drunken nights together, you may find they get on each other's goat.

Fun things to do with your satyr

- *Go on double dates—satyrs are a good way for young, lonely owners to get to know more girls. It can introduce you to nymphs, which are minor, but beautiful, deities, or ask the Nereids around, which are sea goddesses that don't wear bikinis.*

- *Try taking your satyr to Alcoholics Anonymous—everyone will think they have been drinking.*

- *Suggest he performs at girls' nights out —the satyr likes to play the pipes and dance. Half-naked, he makes a perfect entertainer.*

Distinguishing feature: a very keen eye for the main chance.

Where's the party?
A satyr will be only too ready to help you make new female friends, but it can get on the goat of some ladies.

How to live with a …

GORGON

*W*ith some pets, just one look is all that it takes. However, love at first sight isn't going to happen with a gorgon, for two reasons. First, gorgons are, frankly, pretty ugly; startlingly hideous might be going too far, but only just. And, second, if you look one in the eye, you could be turned to stone. Their appearance will certainly make heads turn in the street, but their gaze is petrifying. This is one pet that can stop people dead in their tracks.

Character

The name derives from the Greek for "terrible," *gorgos*, and suits it perfectly. Choose from different varieties: two of them, Sthenno and Euryale, who are immortal, and a third, Medusa, who suffers the ravages of time. Once beautiful, all the sisters were made hideous by the outraged goddess Athena, when the sea god Poseidon seduced Medusa in her temple. Furious, she turned ringlets to serpents, and gave them teeth a wild hog would find embarrassing, plus the power to petrify any mortals foolish enough to look them in the eye. As revenge goes, it was pretty comprehensive, and made the gorgons the terrifying, if shy, queens of the underworld.

Appearance

Aboard the shoulders of a woman's body sits a broad, round head, enveloped by writhing, serpentine hair. Huge eyes stare out of its face, two nostrils flare, and hoglike fangs and tusks protrude from a gaping mouth, embracing a long, lolling tongue. It has brazen-clawed hands and wings on its back. Move over, gargoyle.

• Gorgon
(Gorgos Nongorgeous)

What you need

• **A comfortable apartment for your pet.** It must include everything a demanding girl could want, and a few things a snake needs. If your pet has semiaquatic snakes for hair, then let it chill by the pool, and the snakes can enjoy a bit of a splash at the same time. Never let her see her reflection in the pool. She ain't Narcissus.

• **A lack of reflection.** All mirrors and reflective metal surfaces need to be covered up in order to keep your pet safe from its own reflection. Beauty may be in the eye of the beholder, but in the case of a gorgon, you will need sunglasses to appreciate it.

• **A snake-charmer.** To try to keep your gorgon's hair in some semblance of order. A hairdresser won't have the first idea how to tease her tresses.

> *The pet that has a bad hair day every day.*

Good night
Accommodate her dual needs. She can relax on her custom-built aqua-recliner and let sleeping snakes lie at the same time.

Table manners
Be watchful of your gorgon over dinner, but from behind dark glasses, or you could see the tail end of your relationship.

Feeding habits

The gorgon is no feast for the eyes, but it has the teeth for one. It can eat pretty much anything it lays its clawed hands on, or that you might care to serve it. An intimate dinner à deux might not be the romantic occasion you would hope, however: its fangs are fierce, so it will be able to masticate most foods, but the lolling, often vibrating, tongue can get in the way sometimes and can be very off-putting when you are eating. Try to feed the snakes first; that way they won't wind up pinching food off your pet's plate, or, indeed, yours. Candlelit dinners are out because you will be wearing shades.

Veterinary care

All practitioners will need appropriate protection from the petrifying powers of your pet, plus some specialist skills. You will require a veterinarian keen on reptiles and capable of checking them for mites and ticks on a regular basis while advising on how to control their body temperature, given their unusual habitat. You will also need a doctor, female preferably, to handle the human side of things. The gorgon will also require a rock-solid dentist, given the nature of the beast. It will need to floss fangs and tusks regularly.

Fun things to do with your gorgon

• *Turn your least favorite people into handsome statues—get your pet to turn the traffic cop who's given you three tickets, or the pedigree dog that keeps messing on your lawn, into striking garden ornaments. Your friends will be amazed at the lifelike detail, all executed in genuine stone.*

• *Offer its services as a team mascot—equip your team with sunglasses and watch them kill the opposition stone dead. Game over.*

• *Get help for your mail shot—the gorgon is great at licking postage stamps and envelopes.*

Companion pets

The gorgon is not gregarious. Its ancestors used to hide in the obscurity of the underworld guarded by three siblings, the Graeae, so you could try to track down some of their descendants. Perpetually old, these women share an eye and a tooth between them. The sisters might enjoy the odd party game of "blind woman's buff." You would be unwise to ask a basilisk over, given its own deathly stare.

Frozen art
At a glance, your pet can help you to enlarge your contemporary-art portfolio and reduce your pet hates.

Key skill: creating contemporary art with ancient techniques.

How to live with a ...

LAMIA

*T*he lamia is not suitable for everyone. **Originally from the Libyan desert, and part-woman, part-serpent, it can assume the shape of a wholly beautiful woman on occasion. It actively dislikes men and children. In fact, it dislikes them so much it will lure them to their doom and eat them. To own this pet, therefore, women only need apply.**

Character

The original, beautiful lamia was one of the many loves of the übergod Zeus, and mother to a number of his offspring. When his consort, Hera, discovered their affair, she transformed the lamia into an ugly woman-serpent and killed as many of the children as she could find. Taking revenge on the gods wasn't an option, so the lamia turned to lesser mortals, targeting both men and children and devouring many of each. Incapable of normal speech, the lamia makes its views on the young and the male abundantly clear in other ways. Its musical whistle lures many a male traveler to his doom.

• Lamia
(Lamya Exfoliata)

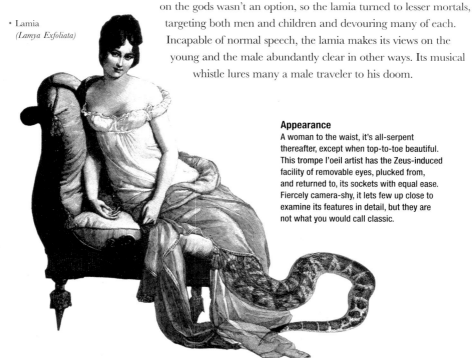

Appearance

A woman to the waist, it's all-serpent thereafter, except when top-to-toe beautiful. This trompe l'oeil artist has the Zeus-induced facility of removable eyes, plucked from, and returned to, its sockets with equal ease. Fiercely camera-shy, it lets few up close to examine its features in detail, but they are not what you would call classic.

What you need

• **A clothes stylist.** Your lamia will need expert advice on what to wear and what not to wear, given the demands of its extraordinary figure. It has beguiling, snakelike hips, but the lower half is definitely not its best asset and needs particular attention, and clever disguise. Remember, snakeskin designs would be overkill.

• **A long bath.** Standard baths will not accommodate the lamia, with its serpentine proportions. Install a luxurious bath of unusually long dimensions in which it can unwind properly, or let its tail drape over the end.

• **Yoga classes.** Your lamia needs to stay in shape, keep flexible, relax, and heal deep-rooted anger that goes way back. Yoga could help, and it already has the Bhujangasana (snake pose) under its belt, naturally.

> *The ultimate premodernist, feminist pet.*

Pet love
Single, childless, female pet-owners, who think all men are snakes, will love the lamia. You might have to fight for the bathroom.

Important physical feature: scaly, serpentine extremity.

Radical skincare
Your pet enjoys to be
pampered. Snakeskin-oil
salesmen are not required
or permitted. This is strictly
a "girls only" boudoir.

Feeding habits

Never say "Have what you want" to a hungry lamia. If offered the chance to
go à la carte, it would select children as an appetizer and men as an entrée.
It is up to you to make sure that anthropophagy is not on the menu. Dishes
can be carnivorous and can even appeal to the cannibal in your pet, if in
name only. Try offering her child-size portions, bite-size fish fingers, whole
baby kid, or leg, neck, and shoulder of young lamb to divert her from, and
compensate for, her taste for the real thing. It might even be fooled by the
odd sheep's eye. Never let it dine out in a restaurant.

Veterinary care

A female veterinarian is the only option for a lamia. Ancient pet manuals record graphically how male attendants have come and gone, the way of all flesh. A female practitioner can attend to your pet's feminine needs and advise on hair- and skincare. Find a skillful makeup artist who will put on a brave face at your home. She can suggest ways of exfoliating and moisturizing for the top half; the lower half will take a more radical approach to removal of dead skin.

Companion pets

Its necessarily restricted social life will impact your own. You would be ill advised to ask male members of your family, or indeed any male friends, colleagues, or suitors, back to your place, unless you wanted the lamia to give them the elbow. Children of any kind must be kept well away from your companion. If you have the facilities, you could ask a mermaid and a siren over, and they could swap their notes about how to seek out, lure, and destroy all men.

Fun things to do with your lamia

- *Sell your pet's life story to the* National Enquirer/*gutter press—when the male journalists doorstep your home, let your lamia meet and greet them.*

- *Suggest it makes a follow-up movie with Hannibal Lecter—write to the producer and suggest it be called* When Hanny met Lammy.

- *Invite your ex-husband over to meet your new friend when in "total woman" mode—wait for her to change back into man-eating woman-serpent over the cheese and crackers.*

How to live with a ...

MANTICORE

*B*efore you fall for this human hybrid, part furry lion, part big-eyed man, you should know that the manticore, also known as martikhora, derives its name from the Old Persian word for "man-slayer." Don't be put off, but be aware that this pet is quite a handful, if not a mouthful. It has far more than its fair share of teeth, a voice like a pipe-and-trumpet mix, and an endless supply of poisonous quills in its tail.

• Manticore
(Martikhora Manslaya)

Appearance
The strong body of a lion, with blood-red fur and mane, is very nicely offset by the crimson, bearded face, and ears, of a man. Piercing, blue-gray eyes stare out of its face, slashed by a large mouth sporting a triple-decker dental display. The scorpionlike end of its tail bristles with a self-replenishing supply of foot-long, deadly spines.

Character
Hailing from India, it was first chronicled by Ctesias of Cnidus, who served in the 5th-century CE Persian courts. One was presented to the Persian king, but records don't reveal if he looked his gift manticore in the mouth before accepting it graciously. It is as swift as a stag, with a powerful, agile, leonine physique, a naturally wild temperament, and an unusual, somewhat

worrying, taste in men and women, for whom it lies in wait before slaying them with its quills then devouring them in their entirety. It is also capable of speech, but do not indulge in barbed comments of your own.

What you need

• **An inventive interior designer.** The manticore has a schizophrenic lifestyle, so accommodation should be "domestic wilderness" in design, but also robust and functional, offering traditional human comforts, complete with enormous backyard and outdoor dining area.

• **Full-body armor.** This should include shield, helmet, and visor for when you first bring your baby manticore home and begin the bonding process. Things could cut up a bit rough during early controlled play sessions with your baby manticore, and later teenage ones.

• **An elephant.** The only animal that has a hide thick enough to survive the deadly spines from your pet's tail. If you fancy getting up close and personal with your manticore on a wild-eyed, bad-hair day, do so aboard an elephant.

> *A pet with more 'agh' than 'aah' factor.*

Riding high
Only an elephant has the spine for your pet's poisonous quills. Hitch a ride on its unpetrified hide for your own safety.

Veterinary care

You will need several professionals to attend to your manticore. Hands-on care by a big-game veterinarian is going to be possible only after some face time with a therapist who can help your pet with its eating disorder. Once the sting has been taken out of its tail and it has kissed goodbye to its inner cannibal, recruit the services of a dentist and a barber. They may keep your pet at arm's length for a while by using drills and razors with enormously extended handles.

Right-arm tactics
Some dentists would give their eye teeth to treat a manticore. The jaws of others would drop at the sight of one.

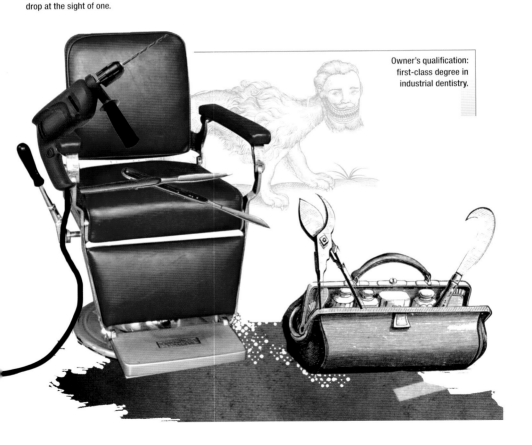

Owner's qualification: first-class degree in industrial dentistry.

Feeding habits

Although it has the front to be a cannibal, you can try to fight a rearguard action against this terrible, tasteless tendency. A manticore's gut instinct is carnivorous; it can quite happily subsist on a rich diet of buffalo, giraffe, zebra, or wildebeest, and its claws and quills make it entirely self-sufficient. However, its more antisocial appetites need to be controlled by diversion therapy. Provide alternative, tempting menus. Appeal to the lion in it with the living, breathing, fresh-off-the-shelf meat counter that is the safari park. If it trumpets a demand for alcohol, never let it touch a drop—things could really fly off the handle (or tail).

Companion pets

Although the elephant can survive a close encounter with a manticore, this does not make it a willing friend or a natural companion, and any conversation would be frustratingly one-sided. It might find its match in its equally fierce, part-man, part-tiger equivalent—the lympago. They could chat about their shared challenges and concerns as hybrids. It might enjoy the odd phone call with a centaur, but face time is best taken off the menu.

Fun things to do with your manticore

- *Host parties—once tamed, it makes a wonderful entertainer at parties, regaling guests with tales of its ancestors, doing impressions of them, or providing background music during the evening, all at a suitably safe distance from your possibly nervous guests (or not, depending on how much fun you want to have).*

- *Enter your manticore into an archery competition—it can fire its quills straight ahead by bending its tail over its body, or shoot them backward with its tail fully outstretched. Once launched, they are replaced. Bullseye.*

How to live with a …

SELKIE

*M*ost pet-care manuals stress that pets are for life, not just for Christmas. But the selkie is different. Very different. Shapeshifter extraordinaire, it can transform itself from seal to human, shedding its skin as it emerges from the sea on to the shore. With similar ease, it can resume its marine mammal form by donning its sealskin once more, returning whence it came. This pet is on loan from the sea. You have to prove you are worth your salt as its guardian.

Character

Also known as selchies, silkies, and roanes, they hail originally from the Orkney and Shetland islands (*selkie* means "seal" in the Orkney dialect), but they also lived in Ireland and Iceland. Shy, solitary, gentle, and understanding, they can fathom both the depths of the salty blue and your emotions. Once you have earned its trust, it will become a close companion. Male owners might be tempted by the female's reputation as an excellent, if wistful, wife, but should beware its marine husband. The seductive power exerted by male selkies over human women makes them a handful. Girl selkies come recommended.

Appearance

In its human form, the female selkie is slim, graceful, and lithe. It has long, dark, pretty hair; pale, soft, unblemished skin; large, deep-brown, soulful, expressive eyes. A beautiful creature, it comes with an exotic touch—webbed toes and fingers. Its delicate thorax contains fine lungs that endow it with extraordinary underwater abilities.

• Selkie
(*Sigillum Sexyium*)

What you need

• **A pleasant home in an unspoilt coastal location.** Your pet is of Scottish ancestry, and its ideal habitat would be an island in cooler, nontropical climes, with unpredictable weather and large supplies of fish. It enjoys meditating and relaxing on outlying rocks, and dancing on moonlit, lonely shores. Hearing the sea in the distance will remind it of home. City-apartment-owners and desert-dwellers should not fantasize about a selkie.

• **Respect.** You will need to keep the sealskin very safe. If it is lost or stolen, your pet is doomed to remain in human form and might even have to marry a male owner, thereby committing bigamy. Damaging or hiding it would be an unforgivably cruel act.

Wave goodbye
Your selkie likes to spend time by the sea, thinking of home. Desert-dwellers should think again.

> *This is one pet you don't get to keep.*

Feeding habits

Your pet will have an understandably pronounced penchant for the piscatorial. When sea-based, the pinniped's diet comprises fish, squid, octopus, and small crustaceans, all enjoyed so raw and fresh they are still quivering. When it is land-based, the selkie's appetite will embrace a variety of cooked or smoked fish, a little meat, some fruit, and the odd portion of steamed samphire. It is not used to alcohol and could become horribly homesick if allowed to drown its sorrows. Some selkies find holding cutlery difficult, given their webbed fingers. Chopsticks are an option. Why not enjoy a shrimp and squid stir-fry al fresco on the beach, while listening to the lapping waves on the not-too-distant shore?

Veterinary care

When land-based, your selkie will naturally be in its human form, so a doctor will be the appropriate consultant for any complaints. Choose an understanding general practitioner, one who can appreciate your pet's subaqua past and the shape of its future. Find discreet chiropodists and manicurists in order to avoid news of your selkie's unusual extremities being spread on the web. Consult a trusted fur expert from time to time to check that the sealskin is being stored in the right conditions.

Companion pets

The selkie-human is a retiring soul. It joins other selkie folk for moonlit beach discos, but has few close friends from other species. It may enjoy a midnight swim with a mermaid, and the opportunity to compare notes on top-to-tail beauty routines and keeping hair briny-shiny. The mermaid is a much darker and moodier creature, and a bit of a party animal, and they are unlikely to become bosom pals. They do share a horror of krakens, however.

Fun things to do with your selkie

- *Take it on a Mediterranean cruise—your pet will frolic in the sea during the day and dine at the captain's table at night. Pack black gloves and avoid open-toed shoes.*

- *Go to a gig—selkies love music. Attend a traditional Celtic folk concert, and its eyes will glisten as you listen to songs of the sea. Be prepared for a faraway look and some webbed tapping …*

- *Make waves—challenge the record for underwater breath-holding. Signed, sealed, delivered—the record's yours.*

Take a break
Take an overseas vacation with your selkie. It could teach you to swim during the day and meet up with distant relatives at night.

Distinguishing feature: webbed feet, for surfing not dancing.

How to live with a ...

FAIRY

*W*hen considering the entries in this manual, you may find some of them unbelievably challenging at first sight. The fairy demands a second sight at least. It won't place an unusual strain on your budget, or cause you to extend your current accommodation; it won't push your culinary skills to their limit either, but it can stretch your credibility and imagination. Fairies live alongside humans quite happily but in a supernatural context. This is a very otherworldly pet, so be wary of a fairy.

Character

"Fairy" (aka faery or faerie) is linked to the Latin for destiny, *fatum*, and the wee folk can influence fate—yours included. Your fabulous choice of fey, enchanted beings includes, in alphabetical rather than size order, djinns, dwarves, elves, gnomes, goblins, nature spirits, pixies, sidhe, sprites, sylphs, and trolls, with a fine range of skills and interests that include fixing, mending, washing, healing, flying, spell-casting, future-divining, meddling with mortals, child abduction, horse-stealing, and shoe-making. They love nature, animals, and flowers, are fond of song and music, and enjoy dancing and feasting at night, unseen by humans. They can be good, very good, or bad, very bad.

• Fairy
(*Faerie Elusivae*)

Appearance

Fairies come in small, medium, and large sizes, and if you can't see them, don't call the optician—they can shapeshift, even into the invisible. Sometimes diaphanously winged and marvelous, they are nebulous, fabulous, and, believe it or not, ubiquitous. Favorite colors: green, red, brown, and earthy hues; favorite fairy fabrics: moss and leaves. Honestly, you ain't seen nothing yet.

What you need

• **Mounds of space.** Fairyland is a place where time doesn't exist, and fairies spend a lot of it. They live underground in mounds or barrows. Unless you just happen to have a prehistoric burial mound on your property, a man-made one will do.

• **A philosophical bent.** Fairies reflect our own deep struggle with the concepts of good and evil, illusion and reality, natural and supernatural, nice and horrid. Does time exist? Do I have a pet or has my pet had me? Answers, like fairies, are hard to grasp, but challenging.

• **Caution.** If you see a fairy ring, made of mushrooms, withered grass, or stones in the wooded area of your property, don't disturb it, or your fairy will cast a spell on you in revenge.

An out-of-this-world pet that has to be believed to be seen.

Fairy rings
Fairy rings demand respect. Trespassers will be transformed. If you fancy life as a frog, then hotfoot it into the magic circle.

Little and large
Goblins are faery folk, too, but less attractive than some. Big as your hand or your horse, they play pranks and have terrible teeth.

Distinguishing feature: short sighted but with unworldly vision.

Feeding habits

There are too many types of little people to give individual dietary advice. However, there is an excellent and comprehensive tome covering all their nutritional needs, and we recommend you invest in a copy of *Natural Food for the Supernatural Pet: What Fairies Eat* at your earliest opportunity. Some enjoy the food of the woods—fruit, nuts, seeds, and berries, washed down with a glass of flower nectar. Those with a sweet fairy tooth enjoy honey. Others are thought to extract the essence from food, leaving the substance behind. Larger humans indulging in too many fairy cakes might like to take a leaf from their fairy tale book.

Recommended diet: 100 percent natural, 100 percent supernatural.

Veterinary care

Your pet will require treatment infrequently, but administering it can be problematic. The only injury it cannot self-treat is accidental harm to the wings. These delicate, diaphanous appendages are difficult to fix, and your veterinarian will need both patience and experience to do so effectively. He or she should be armed with a pair of steel scissors as a spell-repellent (this metal nettles a fairy) before attempting treatment; a frightened fairy in pain could fire off some damaging magic before its wing can be splinted or bandaged.

Companion pets

Fairies have fey friends everywhere. You could invite the selkie over for a shapeshifting soiree. No need to spend hours getting ready, they can change just before the party starts. The leprechaun is an entertaining and useful guest. This male Irish fairy is an excellent cobbler, and although by nature solitary, has a wealth both of fairy tales to tell and buried treasure. Try to get him to bare his soul.

Fun things to do with your fairy

- *Get rich quick—ask your pet to arrange a fairy gold card for you. The sky's the limit. Your bank manager won't credit it.*

- *Get a metal detector—if the leprechaun won't reveal where the treasure he buried is hidden, hire a machine and go hunting for it yourself.*

- *Get Pucked—follow in the fairy footsteps of Puck, in Shakespeare's* A Midsummer Night's Dream. *Cast a spell and watch your ex make an ass of him- or herself.*

BIRDS

$\mathcal{B}$ird lovers can spread out
their wings in this section. It
doesn't get much bigger than
a roc, more dangerous than
a basilisk, more of a challenge
than a siren, uglier than a harpy,
and more eternal than a phoenix.

How to live with a …

BASILISK

A basilisk makes rather specific demands on its owner, and it is not for the faint-hearted. Fully capable of destroying everything in its path by the merest glance, touch, breath, hiss, or, indeed, whiff from its foul-smelling body, it will not suit the fearful, sensitive, or neighborly. However, if you have always harbored an urge for dangerous pet-keeping, and you possess far more than your fair share of courage, negative, destructive, or antisocial impulses—not to mention land— then put the basilisk on your list of pets for consideration.

Character

The word "basilisk" comes from the Greek word for "little king," *basiliskos*, and it certainly lives up to its reputation of lording it over other creatures, with its crown-marked head held at a regal angle and its superior gait, middle coil raised high. No slithering for this small, but perfectly deadly, kingly serpent, from which all other creatures flee like obedient subjects, eager not to be on the receiving end of its fatal gaze, toxic breath, or hydrophobia-inducing hiss. The basilisk has been master of the withering look since its arrival in Ancient Greece and has no plans to change with the times.

Appearance

This mix 'n' match pet is no oil painting. With a cockerel's head, neck, and legs, a serpent's body and tail, and dragon wings, it is surprisingly diminutive, given its hugely aggressive instincts— only 12 inches long—with a bright-white diadem marking on its forehead and sparkling, piercing red eyes.

• Basilisk
*(Basiliskos
Bestialis)*

What you need

• **An extraordinarily large sandpit or small desert.** Its natural environment after rock-splitting and waste-laying activities.

• **A hands-off approach to pet-keeping.** You can't cuddle, stroke, or hug your basilisk.

• **No social life.** You won't be popular with friends, neighbors, or visitors, but your basilisk will keep you on your toes.

Split personality
Your basilisk can rend rocks and raze grass with just one glance. Tops the pecking order of "slash and burn" pet birds.

• **A large mirror for extreme measures.** Looking at its own reflection can be fatal, and is one of only three ways of controlling a basilisk, as St. George discovered when he turned his shiny shield toward one and felled it.

• **A weasel and a rooster.** These are important if your mirror goes missing. Basilisks are terrified of weasels, and suffer fatal convulsions when they hear the crow of a cockerel or rooster.

The pet of choice for the friendless.

Key skills: ear-, nostril- and rock-splitting abilities.

Feeding habits

The basilisk dines outdoors like a destructive king; it has no competition for food, deterring it with its unique range of death-inducing threats and techniques. Once it has reduced all that it surveys to rubble and waste, it will move to a new section of your generous property, having rotted the fruit off the trees and poisoned the drinking water for centuries to come. Feeding by hand is a very bad idea: the basilisk's fatal venom can pass through the food into your palm, as an ancient knight discovered after wounding a basilisk and subsequently succumbing, along with his horse, to the deadly poison that traveled back up his spear.

The sky's the limit
The basilisk can charm
the birds from the sky.
The only trouble is they
are stone dead before
they hit the ground.

Veterinary care

The inevitable fascination that such a fabulous hybrid pet will hold for your local veterinarian will be stopped dead in its tracks by the fear of meeting its gaze or inhaling its body odor, and in such an event he or she would need to be replaced almost instantly. You could try the new veterinarian in town, who didn't study Ancient Beasts, if you are feeling particularly destructive. However, ensuring weasels, mirrors, and roosters are kept safely under lock and key for emergency use only, you shouldn't require his or her services. This is a pretty self-sufficient companion.

Companion pets

Sadly for the basilisk, it has no known natural companions. Practically "incompetible" with others, it does have a close relative, but you would be ill-advised to ask it over to play: the cockatrice, a winged reptile hatched for nine years from a seven-year-old cockerel's egg by a toad, has the same antisocial reputation for instantaneous death. You will have your hands full with one basilisk, thereby dispensing with the need to find a basilisk partner for your pet.

Fun things to do with your basilisk

- *This is the ultimate guard beast—an illustrated "Basilisk lives here" sign will deter anyone, even the boldest intruders.*

- *If your boss is threatening to sack you, suggest you have a "Bring Your Pet to Work" day—that should stir things up nicely.*

- *Make some extra money by offering the services of your basilisk to a demolition company or one needing help in tunneling or quarry work—when they flee in terror, take over the company.*

How to live with a …

SIREN

$\mathscr{H}$ybrid-bird fanciers can decide between the harpy and
the siren on the semifeathered-friend front. Those desiring
something easier on the eye and nose will probably plump
for the siren. This bewitching, and sweeter-scented, avian-
girl may well strike the right note with the musically inclined
birder. Its lovely voice is deceptive, however. In ancient times,
its mellifluous, mesmerizing melody promised
omniscience, but delivered death, luring sailors
to a watery grave. Don't let it pull the plug on
your future. Make sure you remain captain of
your own pet-keeping fate.

Appearance
This seductive sea nymph looks
like a harpy after a full-body
makeover and radical surgery.
No crow's feet, but instead the
lovely face of a girl perched
upon a fine female torso, a
below-the-waist bird's body,
with gold and reddish plumage,
claws for feet, both wings and
arms, and vocal charms.
Some models sport fishtails.

• Siren
(Syrene Serene)

Character

This semibird can charm the real thing from the trees, and the gullible
guys from their Greek galleons, with its honey-sweet, hypnotic harmony.
Its parentage is much debated; it is thought to be the offspring of Achelous,
depicted in some manuals with a bull's head and body, plus fishtail, and a
Muse, hence the sweet song. It has a special connection with southwestern

Italy after years spent on the island of Aeaea, beguiling and devouring at whim. Many mortals have been strung along by its charms, their futures wrecked on rocks, along with their heads and bodies.

What you need

• **A secure, sea-less home.** Avoid islands, and you will save the life of many a seafarer. Accommodate your siren in an environment enclosed by land and other subtle, but effective, measures; keep a close eye, if not ear, on it; and restrict contact with visitors who are not classically versed in the art of siren-keeping.

• **Lots of beeswax.** It saved Odysseus from an ancient fate worse than death. While he was lashed to the mast of his ship, he stuffed it in the ears of his crew as they rowed past a siren. Keep a supply on warm hand for emergencies.

• **A discerning ear.** Learn to filter the noise from the news. Your siren can vocalize very strong views, and promise you great knowledge. Omniscience isn't everything, after all. It can be dead boring.

> ❝ *Fall for this pet at your peril—you may have to drown your sorrows.* ❞

Bee's knees
Should the odd sailor pop by, your own production line of beeswax will prove to be a vital accessory.

Feeding habits

The siren has an unfortunate taste for sailors. Unwitting seagoing souls were lulled into a state of high insecurity by its song, torn apart, and tastelessly devoured. Others would leap into the waves to join the singer-siren and drown. It was a pretty effective way of getting a very fresh take-out with organic salt. Teach your nymph-with-maniac-tendencies proper table manners. Supply a more varied diet. Five-a-day should involve seeds and fruit, not seafaring men. Help it develop a taste for a more, or less, human diet. During early dîners à deux, keep ear wax on hand and play loud music to drown out dangerous ditties.

Veterinary care

Recruit a waxed-up veterinarian who makes a beeline for birds in his career, together with a hard-of-hearing or short-sighted general practitioner; both should be blind and deaf to your pet's dangerous allure when tending to its feathers or frailties. The siren is not a natural or easy patient and cannot be treated on a wing and a prayer, although either might be the answer if things get really difficult. Macho medics wanting to get their hands on a beautiful bird may have their hopes dashed.

A trio of brio
Build a studio for your pet and invite the sisterhood over to make music. You could all enjoy some killer hit records.

Fun things to do with your siren

- *Kamikaze karaoke—enter an outdoor singing competition from on board a boat when on vacation, and watch your siren drown out its rivals as they plunge seaward.*

- *Form a girl band—invite two of its siblings to live with you and form a pop group. Call it The Three Degrees of Separation.*

- *Hold a fashion show—if your siren has a fishtail, invite the mermaid and the selkie over to see what everyone is wearing on the piscine waterways this year.*

Hit the right note
Sirens like nothing better than a sea-based sing-off. No chance of a dead heat. Wave a fond farewell to the competition.

Important physical feature: vocal chords to die for.

Companion pets

There is some dispute as to how many sisters the siren has. Anywhere from one to four, it seems. Each enjoys a good aria as much as the next siren, accompanied by a spot of lute-playing. Gather them together for a classical-music soiree. You won't be able to ask anyone else to join in for fear of repercussions, though.

How to live with a ...

PHOENIX

*T*his is the ultimate in exclusive and fabulous pets. Only one phoenix exists at a time, anywhere in the world, making it just about as unique as it gets. This visually stunning firebird, with its extraordinary plumage and powers of eternal regeneration, is the perfect companion for those who appreciate visual beauty, enjoy heart-stopping birdsong, own the kind of paradiselike property that befits the phoenix's beauty, and can arrange for continuity of care for this quintessentially "eternal" pet.

• Phoenix
(*Phoenix Phirex*)

Appearance
The eaglelike phoenix derives its name from the Greek word for purple-red, *phoinix*. Its head, breast, and back are covered in feathers of this luxurious hue, and offset by iridescent wings, an azure tail, and a striking ruff of gold around the neck. It sports a somewhat unusual tuft of feathers behind its head.

Character

Most pet-care manuals from the 5th century BCE put the lifespan of the phoenix at 500 years (some say up to 1,460.) They describe how, when it feels old, it builds a nest of aromatic branches, sets it alight, is consumed, and, three days later, is completely reborn from the ashes. Until then, the average phoenix's day goes like this: rise at dawn, bathe, stretch magnificent wings, and greet sun with delightful song. It is a bit of a home bird, preferring to stay in one place most of the time.

> *The perfect match for the lonely aesthete.*

Single date
This is one bird that takes "going out on a date" literally. You can't palm it off with any other tree.

What you need

• **A date-palm tree.** It will build its pyre there.

• **Sweet-smelling spices.** It will use spices such as cinnamon, and aromatic branches, to make its pyre.

• **Enormous patience.** The waiting list is unbelievable.

• **Tight security.** Just one feather from the phoenix is said to guarantee immortality. Beware representatives from cosmetic companies and Hollywood actresses bearing gifts.

• **Good genes.** A fertile family of phoenix-loving descendants is important, as it is certainly not just for Christmas.

• **An aerial map of the world.** The phoenix has to head off to Heliopolis in Egypt every 500 years to place the ashes from the pyre on the altar of the Temple of the Sun.

Feeding habits

There is some debate about the dietary requirements of the phoenix, not least because it is so circumspect when eating—it will not indulge in front of humans. The most important thing to remember is that it will not kill for food or dine on corpses. It is thought to quench its thirst with dew, subsist on the atmosphere itself, and enjoy the juice of aromatic herbs. None of these, however, should pose too great a demand on the owner.

Veterinary care

After the initial, and not insubstantial, financial outlay that is involved in creating a perfect pad for your pet, you will be relieved to hear that it is inexpensive to care for. Its powers of recovery and regeneration when ill or wounded will keep visits to a veterinarian and any resulting bills to an absolute minimum. Indeed, you may never have to look up the address of the surgery. However, the immortality of the phoenix demands good medical, if not life, insurance on your part.

Companion pets

Loneliness and goodbyes are inevitable issues for the phoenix; it neither requires, nor can have, a mate. It has no relatives, and will outlive other mortal creatures, and, indeed, its owners. It has to start relationships all over again every few decades. However, it is peace-loving, clever, and wise, and should get on with most like-minded beings. Contact with fire-breathing dragons and other pyromaniacs should be restricted to avoid premature regeneration.

Distinguishing feature:
timeless beauty.

Fun things to do with your phoenix

- *Make your friends deeply envious by having regular facelifts—tell them a little bird told you the name of a fabulous surgeon.*

- *When your phoenix prepares its pyre, ask over an old flame who dumped you—enjoy sweet revenge when they look back in horror as your phoenix flutters in the flames of an open fire.*

- *Save on electricity and heating bills—turn off the lights on a winter evening and enjoy the subtle, warming glow with which your phoenix illuminates the room.*

Budget bird
A creature of habit, it likes to stay home, and lays the best pyre in town. Heart- and hearth-warming stuff for a phoenix-owner.

How to live with a ...

ROC

*R*oc enthusiasts are largely specialists, and almost as rare as roc's teeth. The real point of this bird is its size. It's huge. So enormous, that unless you are glimpsing it from some distance, you are unlikely to get an all-round view. Close up, you will see details: an immense feather, an unspeakably vast claw, or, more than a little ominously, a beak the size of an automobile. These are the big facts. Own with care. Or don't own at all. Read on and decide.

• Roc
(Rukh Pukh)

Character

The roc, also known as the rukh, is a bird of prey, so its temperament is not unlike that of an eagle—predatory, fierce, a keen hunter, and a loyal mate and parent. On an unimaginable scale, however, and first recorded on the second voyage of Sinbad, the sailor, is its egg, which is 50 yards around. And that's just the egg. The character of the roc necessarily takes second place to its fabulous size. A temperament that might be manageable in a common-or-garden eagle becomes much more of a challenge when its owner is around 100 feet high. You need to decide if you are ready to embrace it.

Appearance
The roc defies detailed description. It is just way too big for words, making it hard to attach descriptions such as "elegant" or "appealing" to it. With vast claws, a boat-size beak, and an almost immeasurable wingspan, it is certainly awe-inspiring in flight. Owners won't have much time to admire its particular features.

We're talking big
It's hard to imagine owning a pet bigger than a small zoo. Make sure you do your research. Don't own one on just a wing and a prayer.

> " *A pet that refutes the big idea that size doesn't matter.* "

What you need

• **A huge tract of unspoiled land, preferably an island.** Keep it in an area so vast that it is unlikely to disturb others, where it can uproot trees for its nest, and where the odd herd of elephants will not be missed. Think Jurassic Park with birds.

• **A strong nerve.** Rocs are their own birds and unlikely to refer to you on the finer points of their behavior. You won't be able to control yours, so you will need to be able to brazen it out should there be an accident.

• **A secure nest.** Its egg would be the ultimate prize for the intrepid collector. Commission a suitably secure nesting box, or adapt the biggest building on your property for the purpose.

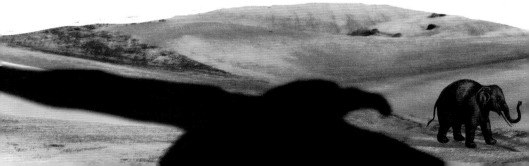

Feeding habits

A roc feeds its young on elephants. Its own tastes have not been well documented, but you should think big, just as it does, however bird-brained. A feast to a roc is a small herd: a whole sheep or cow is little more than a snack, and a whale would be a sashimi platter. Your dilemma is not what to feed your roc, but how to keep up with its elephantine appetite. It doesn't go in for fancy sauces, so there will be no need to cook. It likes its meat bloody, is a skilled hunter (and fisher), and can catch its own. All you need to serve is the raw material.

Lunch is served
Like many modern mothers, female rocs are responsible for bringing home the bacon.

Recommended diet: elephant (single), elephants (plural), herd of elephants (collective).

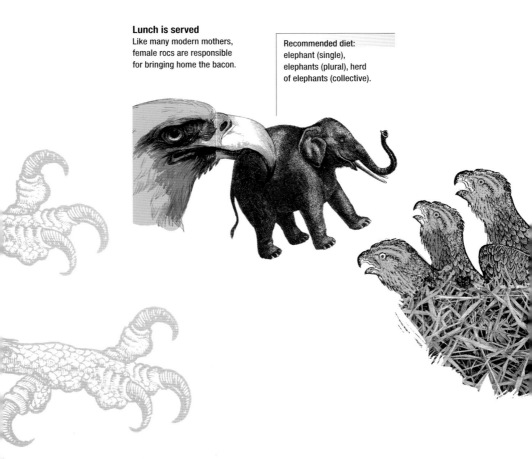

Veterinary care

Care of any kind will have to be administered with caution and a certain distance. If your roc appears to be out of sorts, consult an avian veterinarian with a specialty in birds of prey and a big-game license. Drugs are usually administered with a gun. Amounts, like your roc's body weight, will have to be estimated. More adventurous veterinarians won't hesitate to be a doc to a roc. After all, they will be able to dine out on the story for years to come.

Fun things to do with your roc

- *Run mystery tours—Sinbad tied himself to its leg with his turban, but you can slot customized pods on to its talons. Rocs are alleged to visit valleys full of diamonds, so you might strike lucky.*

- *Reinvent sculpture—blow a roc's egg (with its permission and oil-drilling equipment), paint it, and enter the Venice Biennale with your "eggstract" art piece.*

- *Practice megafalconry—attach dead cattle to a heavyweight truck and drive (very fast) past the roc's resting place.*

Companion pets

Although the phoenix may be a distant cousin, you are advised to keep that distance remote. Indeed, most companions are simply too small to be suitable friends. It would be like a kitten playing with a rhinoceros. However, it's a dedicated family bird and will probably find its own Mr. or Mrs. Roc, and roc juniors will appear like rabbits. Beware, a roc flock is a major, round-the-clock investment.

How to live with a …

HARPY

*J*ust as life can stink sometimes, so can pet-keeping. And to be frank, the harpy reeks. Half haggard-faced woman, half sharp-clawed vulture, it was born to sweep and soar, swoop and snatch. It is always hungry. It is never pretty. It shrieks. Hug, cuddle, or stroke it at your peril. It won't help release feel-good hormones. It doesn't sing. It doesn't dance. And it doesn't look good in photos. But it thieves and abducts—and that's why this pet is a steal.

• Harpy
(Arepyiai Arestinkiai)

Character

The first harpies were of Greek origin, hailing from the Strophades Islands in eastern Thrace. The word *harpyiae* means "swift robber" and, indeed, the harpies were first recruited by the gods to snatch people and objects at high speed. They move faster than any other bird you are likely to meet. They can outstrip a storm, but will excoriate your nostrils with their tailwind. Their droppings contaminate all they encounter. In ancient times, they excelled at torture and preyed on sailors, but that was then, and this is now. Adapt their skills to modern times. Make a harpy work for you.

Appearance
It boasts the head and torso of a woman and the body of a vulture, complete with large-feathered belly. Choose from wide wings and talons of bronze or brass, depending upon your mettle. Its face is always pale, etched with insatiable hunger and foul temper. You will need to look closely for redeeming physical features.

What you need

• **Secure, but attractive, accommodation.** Keep your harpy under lock and key without letting it think it's a jailbird. Once its talented talons become known, your private thief might be stolen, and a bird in the hand is worth two in the bush. Provide a large, lockable aviary, complete with comfortable furnishings, Audubon-pattern drapes, birdy bidet, and a refrigerator with claw-friendly handles.

• **No sense of smell and plenty of disinfectant.** Sadly, there is no getting away from it, your pet has some serious body-odor issues. Use air fresheners, pegs, masks, have nasal surgery—whatever it takes.

• **A large birdbath.** To encourage regular bathing. Frequently check the plughole for feathers.

❝ A pet that can steal a dead heart, if not a live one. ❞

Birds of a feather
Provide all the facilities it could want to lay its greedy claws on. Make its home secure, or it's curtains for you.

Veterinary care

An avian veterinarian will be required to sort out the bird half of your harpy, tending to its talons and keeping its feathers unruffled. You will have to polish its metal wings regularly. If it gets a dose of flu, avian or human, isolate your harpy, tuck it up in bed, let it put up its claws for a while, and keep taking its temperature. You might like to take the opportunity to give it a bit of a makeover, moisturizing its drawn skin and rubbing up its nails.

Home improvements
When your harpy is bed-ridden, give it a bit of a makeover. Start with a bed birdbath. Don't ruffle its feathers too much.

Owner's qualifications: domestic carer cum industrial beautician.

Feeding habits

The harpy eats everything it can lay its brazen claws on. Carrion or roadkill; freshly killed, deliberately raw, or expertly cooked fare; human, animal, vegetable, mineral, or barely identifiable; slow-cooked or fast food, eaten on the hoof, on the wing, on the neighbor's barbecue, at a farmer's market, or at a formal banquet to which neither of you have been invited. Cursed with an unquenchable thirst for meal-stealing, the only culture this half-vulture likes is bacterial. Once you have trained it, you won't ever need to shop again: your harpy is an omnivore par excellence and a serial food-shopper that never takes a purse.

Companion pets

The harpy has a number of sisters, at least three, all of whom use terrible scent and dreadful makeup. However, they would probably enjoy the opportunity to get together and talk about the latest fast-food recipes. Why not arrange a harpy birthday party? They can squawk and squeal, and there's no need for you to prepare a meal—they will steal the day. Just point them in the right direction.

Fun things to do with your harpy

- *Get the birders twitching—put the word out that a fabulous new bird has arrived in the neighborhood. Watch them flock, faint, or flee, without even writing "harpy" in their notebooks …*

- *Get promoted—if they won't give you the job you deserve at work, take your harpy to the office and let it speak for you. Its voice will shatter any glass ceiling in town.*

- *Get rid—your harpy can spirit away your worst enemies. Invite them around and say "adieu" at the end of the evening.*

Pet selector

Key	
Eco-impact	
Appearance	
Sociability	
Cost and maintenance	

If you're pressed for time, use this chart as an instant guide to the right pet for you. It's an at-a-glance selector. Not only will it point you in the right direction, it will prevent you from making inappropriate choices.

Unicorn *page 10*	Fueled by grass and moonlight, this is a very low-impact pet.	At the top of its class: the loveliest pet in the canon.	Demanding: has very specific social requirements.	Fiscally inexpensive, but costly in virgins.
Hippogriff *page 14*	Invaluable personal transport at no cost to the environment.	Impressive rather than beautiful; will appeal to heraldry fans.	Fair: gets on well with other equine-based pets.	Eats vermin; cost-efficient. Won't blow the budget.
Pegasus *page 18*	Fuel efficient; no emissions; eco-friendly diet.	High-end magnificence. Make sure you measure up.	Aloof: other creatures may have problems meeting its strong moral code.	Tack may prove expensive ...
Leucrotta *page 22*	An aggressive participant in the food chain; not the most eco-friendly choice.	Eccentric, but may appeal to the indecisive.	Weak: a natural loner with poor personal hygiene.	Potentially high veterinary bills.
Cerberus *page 26*	Fiercely carnivorous, resulting in an unfortunately heavy carbon footprint.	Strictly for the dog-lover; more is more.	Poor: keeps possible friends at bay.	High: careful security and a generous diet are absolute requirements.
Kraken *page 32*	A one-beast marine disaster; single-handed sourer of any oceanic eco-system.	Vast. What else is there to say?	Will fraternize only with monsters too large for it to eat.	Feeds itself; all other factors are out of your hands.

Dragon *page 36*	Possibility of radically reduced heating and cooking bills.	Handsome and colorful rather than elegant.	Limited: too fierce to be really gregarious.	Will need a monstrous budget: both food and accommodation are necessarily very costly.
Yeti *page 40*	Large footprint, but nonetheless carbon-light. A very eco-friendly pet.	One that you will love or hate. Enthusiasts speak highly of its shaggy charm.	Extremely shy and reclusive. Best left to itself.	Low cost, but you will need sufficient land to accommodate its needs.
Bunyip *page 44*	Flooding risk, though, conversely, this may prove eco-friendly in these times of global warming.	Mysterious; no one is sure what it looks like, so it's appropriate for the lover of surprises.	Very poor; has never had, and will never make, a friend.	Relatively high. Privacy and good security essential.
Hydra *page 48*	High pollutant factor through very toxic breath.	Strictly one for the snake-lover.	The heads get along with one another; apart from this, only crabs need apply.	High heating and feeding bills, plus insurance, puts this pet firmly in the higher expense bracket.
Chimera *page 52*	Accidental deforestation is a definite eco-hazard.	Multidimensional and intriguing, although not conventionally attractive.	Only family members should mix with this pet.	The multidiet requirement may prove both demanding and costly.
Ogre *page 56*	Heavy on the environment—a high-impact pet.	All brawn, no brain; what you see is what you get.	Overshadows companions and needs drawing out.	Big all round: big house, big appetite, big bills.
Centaur *page 62*	What this pet lacks in sensitivity, it makes up for in eco-friendliness.	Deceptively sedate; don't be misled.	All-too inclusive—one to watch, unless you are keen on drunken carousing.	Requires plenty of space, vigilant policing, and an open-minded attitude.

Mermaid *page 66*	Easy on the environment ...	... as well as gentle on the eye.	Capricious, but often charming; a flirtation rather than a long-term relationship.	Not obviously expensive, but barrettes, jewelry, and conditioner can all mount up.
Sphinx *page 70*	With a life lived largely inside its head, this pet has little impact upon the environment.	Elegant and unique—a one-off pet for those who like to be different.	A totally teenage sociability: friends one day, foes the next.	Psychologically taxing, but not particularly expensive to run.
Minotaur *page 74*	The labyrinth creates a micro-climate around this pet; otherwise it has little impact on the environment.	Quite attractive, if bovine's your thing.	Too irascible to be a good mixer.	Lavish feeding is necessary to avoid cannibalistic tendencies; otherwise, few major expenses.
Satyr *page 78*	Mixed impact; when it has too many drinks it won't care about the damage it wreaks.	Energetic, virile, and with a certain appealing charm.	Undiscerning—gets on with everyone.	As exhausting as a houseful of teenagers: the main cost will be to your nerves.
Gorgon *page 82*	Various: the gorgon's ecological impact depends on the direction in which it gazes.	A face that only a mother could love.	Don't even think about it.	An extremely stressful pet. You will need a good insurance policy.
Lamia *page 86*	Too busy cannibalizing humanity to have much effect on the environment.	Changeable—beautiful one day, hideous the next.	Fine with female feminists. This is definitely a pet for those with only XX chromosomes.	An unusual degree of seclusion is required, but need not be costly.
Manticore *page 90*	Can be damaging: its eating habits are not selective. Avoid rare breeds.	Unbelievably bizarre: it's the perfect pet for the very confused.	Best to stick to penpals only.	You will need a safari park and a relaxed attitude to herd numbers; otherwise, fairly low maintenance.

Selkie *page 94*	A gentle footprint in both of its worlds.	Lovely seal, beautiful woman. What's not to like?	A little remote; best with its own kind.	Won't break the bank, but might break your heart.
Fairy *page 98*	Slight: fairies are friends to the environment.	Variable, but generally delicate and attractive.	Equable, but unreliable. Friendships come and go.	A carefree pet; ideal for the constant traveler.
Basilisk *page 104*	An SUV of a pet. Lethal to the environment. Should have a licence.	Unassuming looks mask a terrible capacity for nuclear-level damage.	Not applicable. No friendship survives.	Pets don't come much more expensive than this.
Siren *page 108*	Very hard on sailors, but soft on the environment.	On the cute side of women-bird hybrids; definitely easy on the eye.	Keen on its sisterhood, with a tendency to flock.	Requires a musical owner, but self-sufficient on all other levels.
Phoenix *page 112*	Environmentally friendly: one fire every 500 years doesn't do very much damage.	Breathtaking: it's the avian equivalent of the unicorn.	A graceful, natural loner, but might warm your heart and your hearth.	Negligible. How much does a date palm cost?
Roc *page 116*	Can create problems. An elephant is a snack to this bird, so imagine what damage a hungry roc can do.	Far too big to take in. You never get to see the whole bird.	Not really relevant. Just as elephants don't make friends with ants, rocs overshadow all potential friends.	If you've got the land, you've probably got the money for a roc.
Harpy *page 120*	Noise pollution caused by its inharmonious voice. Strikes the wrong note in the environment.	An unpleasant face perched on a vulture's body. Not usually loved for its looks.	Loves other harpies, but there is no record of other relationships.	It steals what it needs. You won't need to shop, but you may not be able to lunch in your town again.

Index